BEHIND
THE
ACADEMIC
CURTAIN

FRANK F. FURSTENBERG is the Zellerbach Family Professor of Sociology Emeritus at the University of Pennsylvania. He is the author of many books, most recently *Destinies of the Disadvantaged: The Politics of Teenage Childbearing.*

The University of Chicago Press, Chicago 60637
The University of Chicago Press, Ltd., London

© 2013 by The University of Chicago

22 21 20 19 18 17 16 15 14 13   1 2 3 4 5

ISBN-13: 978-0-226-06607-3 (cloth)
ISBN-13: 978-0-226-06610-3 (paper)
ISBN-13: 978-0-226-06624-0 (e-book)

DOI: 10.7208/chicago/9780226066240.001.0001

Library of Congress Cataloging-in-Publication Data

Furstenberg, Frank F., 1940– author.
Behind the academic curtain: how to find success and happiness
with a PhD / Frank F. Furstenberg.
pages; cm. — (Chicago guides to academic life)
Includes bibliographical references and index.
ISBN 978-0-226-06607-3 (cloth: alk. paper) — ISBN 978-0-226-06610-3
(pbk.: alk. paper) — ISBN 978-0-226-06624-0 (e-book)   1. College teaching—
Vocational guidance—United States.   2. Universities and colleges—
United States—Faculty.   3. Doctor of philosophy degree—United States.
4. Universities and colleges—United States—Graduate work.
5. Career development—United States. I. Title.
LB1778.2.F87 2013
378.1′2—dc23   2013008316

How to Find Success and
Happiness with a PhD

FRANK F. FURSTENBERG

The University of Chicago Press

Chicago and London

CONTENTS

PREFACE

Like many senior professors who have spent their lives teaching in a university, I frequently find myself discussing the possibilities and perils of managing an academic career with graduate students, postdocs, and younger faculty. Despite a large and ever-growing number of studies on academia and "how-to" books and blogs, I am always amazed at how little newcomers know about what goes on behind the academic curtain. Lacking experience in higher education, they are often mystified about the everyday life practices and customs of academic life. Understanding how academic life actually works—not just how it is supposed to work—is, I contend, essential to finding happiness and success once you have a PhD. Some might say that these twin goals are almost contradictory or at least difficult to reconcile. Knowledge of what goes on behind the academic curtain increases the chances of making informed and wise choices, which in turn increase the chances of getting what you want once you have your PhD in hand.

My observations draw liberally from my own experiences, complemented by discussions (sometimes informal interviews) with other academics. For the past five years, I have also diligently read and clipped hundred of articles and reports from the *Chronicle of Higher Education* and *Inside Higher Ed*, the leading publications on academic life. I rely less on scholarly studies and do not intend this book to be a compendium of academic research about academia. Some of that work is useful for gaining an understanding of how academia works, but a lot of it is not particularly relevant to the strategy or practice of managing an academic career. After all, knowing what predicts academic productivity is, at most, of minor interest to any particular scholar trying to complete an article or book. My observations are nonetheless tempered by research findings, which I will occasionally cite, but much of what I have to say reflects what I have learned as a teacher and researcher at the University of Pennsylvania, where I have taught in the Department of Sociology throughout my academic career.

While my position at Penn might qualify me to talk about life in a top-tier academic position, what can I say about academic life across the wide range of small colleges, local universities, community colleges, and public and private universities that make up the huge complex of higher education in the United States? This nation has one of the largest and most diverse set of institutions in the world, made up of almost 4,500 colleges and universities serving over 21 million undergraduates, including those attending two- and four-year colleges. Each year a million and a half students receive associate or baccalaureate degrees.[1] The range in quality of these programs is staggering, as is the quality of faculty life. The stratification in higher education is impossible to ignore and will be a central feature of my account of how academia works: it operates very differently at different levels and types of institutions.

Over the past four decades, I have observed academics working under very different conditions, including faculty from two- and four-year colleges who enjoy little or no support for their scholarly activities. I have participated in a number of department reviews, given colloquia at a huge range of institutions, gotten scuttlebutt from countless conferences and meetings, and come to know faculty members from a wide variety of institutions. My former students are spread about in departments of all types, and their observations have been invaluable in writing this book. I have circulated chapters to friends, students, and colleagues willing to read and comment. You might say that I have been a "participant-observer" in the field of higher education for a very long time.

It would be misleading to potential readers, however, if I did not acknowledge up front that I have a lot more to say in this book about how academia works for those headed for or in a tenure-track position than those who are spending their careers in a for-profit institution, a local teaching institution, or a community college, where job security may be perilous and working conditions less than ideal. Nonetheless, my observations are aimed at academics at all ranks and in varied settings, even if I have more to offer in the way of advice to those who are able to work their way into tenure-track positions or jobs that provide full-time contracts. Looking at the present academic world, it is hard not to believe that this middle class—so to speak—is shrinking, as tenured positions become less of a standard and more of a prize than they were when I entered university life. I will make frequent reference to the growing plight of the academic underclass, who are growing in both number and visibility.[2]

College and university professors consistently rank their occupational satisfaction at the top or near the top when compared with other occupations.[3] That comes as no surprise to most of us in the business because most academics have great freedom in arranging their professional lives, we derive tremendous satisfaction from teaching and mentoring, and we are fortunate enough to spend much of our lives pursuing our intellectual and research passions. Finding fulfillment in academia calls for very different strategies in elite universities and colleges that create demanding but rewarding conditions for producing research and in teaching institutions and colleges that are not designed to promote research and scholarship. Inevitably, many young academics begin their careers believing that they want to do scholarly work but end up gaining their principal gratification from teaching.

Whether a career in higher education will continue to merit a high level of job satisfaction in the future is a topic on which there is much speculation and a lot of disagreement. I am no more competent at crystal-ball gazing than some of my readers. I have seen an enormous amount of change in my own lifetime in how universities are organized and run; there is every reason to expect the relentless bureaucratization of higher education to continue. Tenured positions as a fraction of all academic jobs have been shrinking even as the slots in higher education have grown. Inequality—long a prominent feature of higher education—has increased, widening the distance between the haves and the have-nots. Distance learning, for-profit institutions, state and local controls on higher education, the availability of government funding, and many other forces could change the academic landscape in ways that will alter many of today's truths. Yet the Cassandra warnings of a bleak future for academia are anything but new. Many features of academic life have persisted over the course of the past century and probably will continue to endure through the lives of those who are about to enter academia.

Not that a high-level job satisfaction keeps us from complaining about the chronic discontents of teaching and research. Professors tend to gripe a lot about the stresses and demands of academic life, the absurd requests from university administrations, the lack of seriousness of our students, and an endless list of other discontents. But at least those of us employed in full-time positions and even many part-time academics are still inclined to acknowledge that we have a pretty good work life. Of course, most of these surveys are directed at those who managed to attain some level of success, completing their degree and finding a job in an institution of higher education.[4] The dropouts are relatively invisible. So, too, are the legions of part-time academics, adjuncts, and individuals who scramble to make a living with a PhD by teaching in the secondary market of academia.

Most academics will tell you that getting there—finding a secure position in academic life—is *not* half the fun. Lots of aspiring academics never make it to the finish line. A significant fraction of the more than 400,000 students who are currently enrolled in PhD programs will not complete their degrees. I will have more to say about that problem in the first chapter. But suffice it to say that at least half and probably many more of the entrants to PhD programs never get their doctorate, and of those who do, many who seek academic jobs will not find them. As I will explain in more detail later on, academic life is all about sorting and stratification. PhD programs and academic departments arrange it that way. They are intentionally designed to make fine discriminations in the recruitment of students, the hiring of faculty, and, especially, the retention of faculty. It is not surprising, then, that those who find job security—the winners in the process—are generally content with their lot. For this reason alone, this book is not just about finding success and happiness in academia, but also about what to do if you cannot. There are attractive options for putting a PhD to good use beyond a teaching career in higher education.

If the system of higher education is arranged to sort and shift, it behooves the PhD candidate or the young professor to understand how things work in academic life. Of course, there is no single perspective on this because how things work operates differently across graduate programs in different fields or disciplines, and varies among departments in universities, colleges, and research institutes within a given discipline. Acknowledging this wide variation, I contend nonetheless that we academics have a lot in common. The rigors of graduate training are shared by natural and social sciences and the humanities even if the particulars vary by field. Indeed, my experience working with scholars from a wide range of disciplines in very different settings has persuaded me that many of the issues we face in managing academic life are more common than not. I'll try to point out some of the differences from discipline to discipline along the way, but readers should easily be able to tell which of my observations fit particular circumstances and which do not.

My aim is to take readers through the entire course of academic life, from entering graduate school to the transition to a faculty position, and then up the ranks to what I call "the endgame," which involves different strategies for concluding an academic career. I will take note of the characteristic problems or dilemmas that occur at each stage of an academic career and different ways of adapting to them. I want to provide the reader with what the late sociologist Pierre Bourdieu referred to as "cultural capital," knowledge of how the world works.[5] Following Bourdieu, this knowledge of how to be a successful academic—the beliefs, manners, and practices necessary for accomplishing research, teaching, and becoming a good colleague—is far more available to people who are situated at the top and far less accessible to those at the bottom. My hope is for this book to help level the playing field somewhat and bring this inside knowledge to those who are not necessarily in the loop.

Some time ago, I started explicitly teaching my students about what to expect as they entered the discipline. Sociologists call this process "anticipatory socialization," the things you can learn prior to assuming a particular social role. I suppose I shouldn't have been surprised that students crave insider knowledge and put it to good use when they learn the rules, expectations, customs, hidden understandings, and practices of the academic world. It was more surprising how often assistant professors and even tenured faculty are unaware of characteristic career dilemmas they will face. No one, it seems, ever told them about these issues before they encountered them. Knowing what to expect at different career stages is useful in planning for likely contingencies. And, I submit, adroit planning helps in making wiser, or at least better-informed, decisions.

I've divided this book into three general parts that correspond roughly to the first (pre-tenure), second (post-tenure), and last phases (heading toward retirement) of an academic career. There is more to know about the first phase than the second or third, so I devote three chapters to the pre-tenure part of an academic career and only two to life after tenure. No question about it, the initial stages of academic life are the most difficult to manage, but any associate or full professor can still go on at some length about the problems of managing academic demands, balancing work and family, and making career choices in later life. Indeed, there is predictably far less written about the latter stages of academic life than the early career stages. More senior readers, then, may skip past the earlier chapters and go immediately to their current situation unless, of course, they want to relive their early years or refer the book to their students. Likewise, readers who are contemplating going to graduate school, currently enrolled in a PhD program, or in the early stages of academic life may be less interested in what lies ahead. It may be simply too early to think, much less fret, about these issues. There will be plenty of time to worry about the curses of life after tenure once you have it.

Higher education is what we social scientists call a social institution, an arrangement or blueprint of how things should work even if they don't always work that way in practice.[6] Institutions are typically designed to reproduce themselves in orderly ways, and this is how academia works. It recruits and trains and ultimately allocates individuals in this social system to positions by rewarding individual promise (acceptance into graduate school) and accomplishment (teaching and research) according to certain understandings that are set by particular fields or disciplines. A lot of the rules are taught in graduate school in the form of what constitutes good scholarship, what types of information and skills must be mastered, and so on. Along with this concrete knowledge, there are myriad and subtle ways of thinking that are part of every academic field. There are also customs and practices that are more difficult to acquire given that they are often not explicitly taught. My objective is to tell the reader as much as I can about what goes on behind the scenes so that he or she gains the knowledge and skills to navigate through the maze of institutional rules, both formal and informal. But, as you, the reader, will quickly learn, individuals must navigate their own particular paths, because from graduate school and onward, academic novices must actively decide what they want in the way of an academic career and whether they are situated to get it. Without an accurate reading of your circumstances, it is easy to wander off course. The higher-education trade journals are full of self-revelatory accounts of going astray at different stages, though most missteps occur in the early years, during graduate school and its immediate aftermath.

Graduate school is a good place to begin because academic careers are often set in place by the university one attends and the training one gets. It provides a durable template for acquiring an academic identity and the skills and practices needed for a successful career in higher education. So the first and in many respects the most important question that a reader must ask is: Am I well suited to enter a graduate program and earn a PhD? Graduate school is the starting point for an academic career, but it also provides an entry into many other jobs.

ACKNOWLEDGMENTS

After more than four decades in academic life, I have amassed a huge debt to my collaborators, colleagues, and students. I like to think that this book represents my effort to pay back this debt by drawing on my and their academic experience to shine a light on the different pathways to success and happiness for those who earn a PhD. I have tried to recall all of those persons who made a tangible contribution to this book. Most did so by reading chapters or through conversations and comments. I apologize to those who are not mentioned by name but who have helped me at some point along the way to completion of this book.

My colleagues at Penn have been extremely helpful. Special thanks go to Randall Collins, David Grazian, Kristen Harknett, Jerry Jacobs, Annette Laureau, Sam Preston, and Jason Schnittker, who have either read chapters at my request or provided support and commentary. I owe more than I can say to Patricia Miller, my longtime administrative assistant and dear friend, who has kept my academic life in order for more than a quarter of a century.

Many other friends and colleagues in other universities have generously lent a hand when I asked for help. I am extremely grateful for thoughtful readings from some of my former students, including Janel Benson, Sheela Kennedy, Rachel Margolis, Laura Napolitano, Michelle Poulin, Kristin Turney, and Zoua Vang, as well as E. Michael Foster, Karen Guzzo, Sarah Hayford, and Jessica McCrory Callarco, who have commented on chapters.

In addition, I sent out chapters to a few strategically situated informants who were kind enough to review them: Stephanie Coontz,

Karen Fingerman, Alan Gitelson, Lauren Rinelli, Robert Scott, Mary Waters, and Elliot Weininger.

There are a few very good friends—Howard Becker, Fay Cook, and Larry Gross—who read a draft of the entire book and offered explicit suggestions for revision. Beyond their welcome advice (not always followed), their support for this enterprise was more than I could have ever hoped for. I was also aided by Barbara Ray's skillful editing when the chapters were in an early stage.

At the University of Chicago Press, I have benefited from the tremendous encouragement that I received from Elizabeth Branch Dyson, who shepherded the manuscript through the office of the Press. I am also grateful for the fine editing of the final manuscript by Erin DeWitt.

I received an outpouring of assistance from my family. I especially want to thank the academics in my family—my stepdaughter, Julie Segre, and my nephew, François Furstenberg—for their careful readings of several chapters and their generous encouragement to me as I wrote this volume. Thanks also go to other family members—Fred Gordon, Michelle Segre, and Kathie Dean—for their vigilant eyes in catching errors in the galley proofs. My children, Sarah and Benjamin, have listened to me go on for years about academic life with an unlimited supply of patience and forbearing.

My deepest debt of gratitude belongs to my wife, Nina Segre, who read the manuscript more than once, contributing her excellent ideas and an endless supply of encouragement for this project. There is simply no way of expressing how much I owe to her.

1

ENTERING GRADUATE SCHOOL

If you are thinking about entering a doctoral program, you are not alone. In 2011, according to figures provided by the Council of Graduate Schools, there were more than 600,000 applications solely to doctoral programs where students are aiming to earn a PhD or an equivalent degree. Overall, the chances of being accepted to any given program are about one in four: rates of acceptance vary greatly by the quality of the university and whether it is publicly or privately funded.[1] About one in eight applicants was admitted in the top tier of private universities compared to over one in three of the second tier of public universities, and almost one in two in the lowest rung of doctoral programs that are classified as low-activity research programs.[2]

Applications to doctoral programs have been steadily rising over the past decade, especially among women, who now make up a majority of applicants and acceptances to graduate programs. Overall, more than 70,000 new students entered doctoral programs in 2011; slightly over half of these first-time students were women. These new entrants to doctoral programs make up only a small proportion of the total enrollment of graduate students in PhD or equivalent doctoral degrees, which numbers more than 440,000 students. In 2010/2011, about 63,000 doctoral degrees were awarded, a 50 percent increase above the previous decade.[3] Although slowed a bit by the Great Recession, the United States remains one of the world magnets for higher education, especially graduate education leading to a doctoral degree.

If you are thinking seriously of becoming a professor, completing a PhD is virtually required. I say virtually because some people have entered academia without a doctorate or its equivalent, although this route has become much rarer over time. (There is more latitude to teach without an advanced degree in many professional schools, although here, too, substitute qualifications count for less these days than they once did.) Many people who are ABD (all but dissertation) do manage to find employment in higher education, but they are almost always confined to teaching in two-year institutions or the lower ranks of four-year colleges and universities. This is because in most fields, there is no shortage of highly competent candidates vying for good jobs. The academic marketplace is highly competitive in most academic disciplines, even for positions that are deemed to be less than ideal. Of course, there are many other career options besides an academic career that you can pursue with a PhD, as I will discuss in the next chapter.

Most students are trained at a more prestigious graduate program than the department in which they accept their first job. Or, to put it differently, *nearly everyone will be downwardly mobile when they leave graduate school*. This makes it highly desirable, if not imperative, to attend the highest-ranked program that you possibly can, unless you are not contemplating an academic career, are willing to constrain your future options, or have as a primary goal teaching rather than scholarship. Settling for less early on increases the chances that you will have to settle for less when you look for a job: "Aim as high as you dare" is good advice for most people. In any case, it makes sense to think clearly about your long-term goals and ambitions *before* you enter graduate school, even if you will modify or refine them after you start a program.

In many respects, the biggest decision is the first one: Should you take the plunge and enter a PhD program? Deciding to go to graduate school is not the same process for everyone. Every year a substantial number of students move seamlessly from undergraduate to graduate studies. Indeed, a small proportion of graduate students begin their program as undergraduates, taking courses as they complete their baccalaureate. This is especially true in the natural sciences, where professional commitments typically are formed earlier in life, often before or during college. It may be less true in other fields, where the decision to go to graduate school may come after working for a while after college, even if getting an advanced degree was always a consideration.

I fell in love with academia and wanted to be a professor after I took my first sociology course in college. I remember thinking at the time, "Oh, this is what I want to do the rest of my life." As far as I can tell from observing hundreds of graduate students over the years, I was a bit odd, certainly by today's standards or even by standards of a generation ago when young adults made professional commitments at earlier ages. These days most instead come to the idea of getting a PhD more deliberately and gradually than I did. Like marriage and childbearing, career decisions have become more intentional and deliberate and therefore protracted. Young adults are undoubtedly right to take their time and think about what they are getting into before deciding to go to graduate school.

In this era of a more leisurely transition to adulthood, it is extremely common for students to take some time off after college and explore their career options through practical experience in their chosen field before entering graduate school. This is generally a good idea because students who come right out of undergraduate studies can founder when they discover that they have not fully realized exactly what is involved in obtaining a doctorate degree. The experience of graduate training is really very different from what it takes to earn a bachelor's degree. Much, much more will be expected of you as a graduate student.

Getting a PhD is a big deal, as most graduate students will tell you. First of all, it generally takes a lot of time. Programs vary widely in how long it takes to complete a doctorate, but you can figure that at least five, and conceivably ten, years of your life will be consumed in the process.[4] The length of time required to obtain a doctorate varies enormously depending on the discipline, funding, and the quality of support provided in a given field and the department. Graduate training is generally shortest in the natural sciences and engineering and longest in the humanities and for doctorates of education, with the social sciences falling in the middle. But that is in part because financial aid is more plentiful in the natural sciences and scarcest in the humanities.[5] The more depressing fact is that many who enter a PhD program will drop out somewhere along the way unless they begin and remain utterly committed to finishing their degree and unless they have the necessary support and guidance to see them over the long haul.

And that is only the beginning. Becoming an academic usually involves a lengthy apprenticeship that starts in graduate school but in many fields stretches even beyond the time when you complete your thesis. Many PhDs are not ready to become assistant professors for several years even with a degree in hand, often accepting a postdoc, a research position, or perhaps a teaching position off the tenure track. In many respects, the process is more analogous to medical training than getting a law degree. Even in the natural sciences, few go directly from graduate school into an academic job; in the humanities, generally the process of gaining a tenure-track job can be very protracted.

But first things first: let's consider whether getting a PhD is the right choice for you.

SHOULD YOU GO TO GRADUATE SCHOOL?

How do you know whether you are a good candidate for graduate school, much less an academic life? There are some easy answers to this question, which I'll take up first, and there are many other considerations that can only be answered once you have decided to take the plunge. Assuming financial support—a big issue that I will return to later on in this chapter—here are some pointers for whether you are a good bet for getting a PhD.

A friend of mine some years ago asked me to talk to his daughter, Emily, about whether she should get a PhD in history. Emily was a brilliant undergraduate who had been nominated for a distinguished scholarship to enter a top PhD program. At first, it seemed like a no-brainer, but after talking to Emily, whom I knew pretty well, for an hour or so, I was convinced that she was not ready to get a PhD and probably would struggle in an academic career unless she could overcome some of her undergraduate habits. "I'm not sure that I want to spend my life writing academic papers," Emily told me. "I want to do something more in the real world." That is not necessarily the kiss of death, I explained to her, but as our conversation proceeded, I discovered several other counter-indications for Emily's prospects in graduate school. She had always had trouble finishing her papers, brilliant as they eventually turned out to be. Although she was capable of working on her own, she really preferred working with others. In fact, she explained that she hated competitive situations and suffered when she faced deadlines.

Procrastination is a serious problem if you want to be an academic. People who cannot get their work finished in a timely manner tend to face troubles in graduate school, especially in the later stages of a PhD program. Furthermore, in most academic disciplines, the ability to work independently—often in the isolation of the library, lab, or in the field—is a necessary condition for completing a doctorate. I explained to Emily that being able to manage your time, complete tasks, and regulate your work life is essential to finishing a graduate program and critical to academic success. If she continued to have trouble on these fronts, she was going to have problems in graduate school. Despite my advice that she put off graduate school and work for a while, Emily spent a couple of relatively fruitless years in graduate school before she dropped out to enter a successful career in business. It wasn't a complete waste of time, she later told me, but she found quickly that graduate school was not for her. But for many people who enter graduate programs without the soft skills to get a degree, it takes more than a year or two to discover that they are in the wrong place.

We tend to assume that getting a PhD requires a high level of intelligence or, perhaps I should say, the kind of intelligence that expresses itself in doing well in school. Of course it does, but it takes more than that, as Emily's case illustrates. Doing well as an undergraduate is virtually a necessary condition for entering a PhD program, but it is not a guarantee that you are good material to get a PhD. Students need to have or acquire in graduate school a set of soft skills that support their intellectual capacities. These soft skills may vary somewhat depending on the academic field, but most successful academics must be able to work on their own, take and benefit from critical advice, work simultaneously on several tasks at once, manage setbacks in their work, and be capable of resisting outside pressures that tempt one away from work demands.

My graduate advisor told me many years after I completed my dissertation that he thought I enjoyed life too much to amount to anything as an academic. It is true that even as a graduate student and a young faculty member, at a time when I worked a lot harder than I do these days, I always believed it was important to make ample space for exercise and entertainment—not to mention a family life. But the sentiment that you need to be able to work hard was on the mark. Academic success requires long hours of study, research activities, and lonely time in front of a computer writing up results. Think about how you responded to the challenge of taking exams, but think even more about whether you enjoyed the process of developing projects, implementing them, and writing up the results. If you don't relish these activities, then entering a PhD program may not be for you.

To do well in a graduate program, you must also have a high level of passion, intellectual curiosity, and devotion to a field of study. To be sure, going to graduate school can reinforce these essential proclivities for entering academic life. Without them, much of our work can seem empty and pointless. Not everyone has the good fortune to fall in love with a subject as I did (much less to stay in love with it). And many who do could find their love quashed or extinguished during graduate school or during the early years of an academic career. Still, you really need to feel the fire in your belly, or at least have a steady flame of desire, that keeps you going when you face the inevitable challenges, disappointments, frustrations, and even rejections during graduate school and beyond.

Finally, an essential quality for staying the course is an ability to manage stress. When my non-academic friends tease me about the seemingly idyllic life that I live—teaching a course or two, traveling for research and conferences, and schmoozing with my graduate students—I sometimes bring them up short by asking them to recall how they felt during exam week at college. That is a chronic condition when you enter academia, I explain. It seems that you are always in debt to someone and usually many people at once. A paper or review is past due. A graduate student is waiting to hear from you about their thesis proposal or first chapter. You need to get a letter or several letters of recommendation off. Colleagues are waiting for the portion of the committee report that you agreed to write. And so on. Being a professor or a full-time researcher is definitely not a typical nine-to-five job. And lest you have the fantasy of time off in the summers, in my experience it almost never happens. Most academics are cramming their summer months with research, writing, and often teaching. While we carve out time for fun, I dare say that few of us manage to put our work completely aside for long periods of time. Many American academics are often amazed when they discover that their European counterparts typically take off completely for a month in the summer.

Graduate programs are not very adroit in selecting students with the soft skills required for being an academic. What matters most for admission—and it should come as no surprise—is abundant evidence of intellectual talent. Programs are looking for people like Emily. It is taken for granted that brilliant people, like Emily, will possess the needed soft skills or, at least, will acquire them along the way. This is a questionable assumption. Work habits, character, personal skills—whatever you want to call the package of attributes that individuals bring with them into graduate school—are arguably no less important to success in graduate school and in academic life than the imperative of having a good intellect and, let's say, strong analytic skills and imagination.

It is a tall order to have it all. Most students I see in graduate school enter programs possessing only parts of the package of intellectual aptitude, soft skills, ambition, and devotion to learning a discipline. Graduate school provides a space and time for learning how to gain the missing pieces and for putting them together before going on the job market. Of course, I am assuming here the most obvious part of graduate training: mastering the knowledge and skills to be a biologist, political scientist, classicist, or whatever your chosen field.

Daunting? No doubt, but for those who have the "calling," as the great political economist and sociologist Max Weber described the vocation of science (and, I would argue, other academic disciplines) and the life of a researcher, it can be inspiring, gratifying, and intensely rewarding work. This is not just my biased opinion. A great deal of evidence shows that professors have among the highest rates of job satisfaction of any occupation.[6] Being a professor provides an opportunity to do meaningful work (for those who think of scholarship as meaningful), teach and mentor, and experience a great deal of personal control over your work. In this particular sense, being a successful academic is almost like getting paid to be a creative artist.

Now, if you are not deterred by the demanding list of job qualifications, read on: the next question is where to go and how to get into the program of your choice.

I've already provided the first rule of thumb for selecting a graduate program. Reach as high as you can in the quality of the schools to which you apply. The National Academy of Sciences has a ranking of top programs in most disciplines, and there are other ratings available to you that may be useful in making a list of desirable schools for consideration.[7] The rating system is far from perfect, and you should not take it as gospel. Ratings of departments are conservative and give high weight to past performance, and are therefore somewhat out-of-date by the time they appear. Talk to people in your chosen field, read the descriptions of programs, and find a good fit of your interests with the programs. Overall, the ranking of the program should generally be among the most decisive considerations of where to apply if you are aiming for an academic job. Rarely is there a "single" best department, but there are usually several or more that should warrant your interest.

Of course, there may be particular reasons for settling for less, such as funding, compatibility with the other parts of your life, romantic considerations, quality of life, and so on. I would not dismiss these other considerations, particularly funding or family concerns, but settling for the second (or third) best option could constrain where you will be hired after you complete your degree. One caveat, however: it usually matters little whether you select the program that is rated first in your field versus the third-ranked program. On the other hand, it matters a lot whether you attend a school in the top ten (and depending on the field, sometimes the top five or three) versus a school in the top twenty, and it is far better to go to a school in the top twenty than merely the top fifty. Generally speaking, the higher the quality of your graduate program, the greater your options on the job market.

This may mean that if you are not accepted into a program of your choice, it could be worth waiting and reapplying with a stronger application that might be improved by work experience, a clearer statement of purpose, or a higher score on the Graduate Record Examination (GRE). This test—used to screen applications in verbal, math, writing skills, and disciplinary knowledge—plays a large and perhaps undue role in the selection of graduate students.

My advice to shoot for the top comes with some qualifications. Sometimes it is preferable to be a bigger fish in a smaller pond because you might receive more training, sponsorship, and support if you are a top prospect in a somewhat less prestigious program. For example, you could work with strong and energetic faculty members in a particular subfield in an otherwise less than outstanding department. There are sometimes reasons to choose a less highly ranked program, but you should not be easily persuaded to make that choice.

When I entered graduate school back in the 1960s, most students made their decisions more or less flying blind. I relied strictly on advice from my college faculty mentors. Today most students are also likely to visit department websites, go to professional association meetings, consult with other graduate students, and even enlist the views of faculty outside their own institution. Far more information is available online today, and students are more professional than ever before in making their choices. Every year I get inquiries from students who think they might want to enroll in my department and want to gather as much information as they can about what our department has to offer. Students now can include in their application statements that they are applying to X or Y program because they want to work with certain faculty or enter a particular subspecialty in a graduate program. It is no longer just a sellers' market.

THE APPLICATION PROCESS

Applications usually include a personal statement, academic grades from your undergraduate institution, letters of recommendation, and performance on the Graduate Record Examination. They may ask for writing samples, prior professional experience, or portfolio work, depending on the program. While particular departments or programs may have standard ways of using these materials in making their decisions, the weight given to each varies enormously. Needless to say, the highly ranked departments in a given field have the luxury of expecting their applications to be uniformly strong across these various indicators, but some are more flexible than others in dismissing a less-than-perfect dossier.

Here are some pointers for assembling your application and making it as strong as possible. Let's begin with the most bedeviling part of the application for some candidates, the Graduate Record Examination. Unfortunately, in my view, GRE scores in many graduate departments trump all other suits, even undergraduate performance, although the evidence supporting the practice of privileging GRE scores is controversial. Numerous studies have been done to validate the high priority placed on the GRE, and the evidence that has been mounted for their significance is the subject of great debate among educational researchers.[8] Researchers are not in agreement over just how much the GRE scores uniquely predict success over and above the other parts of the application process.

Nonetheless, GRE scores usually count significantly, so it is in your interest to do whatever it takes to get a high score, whether it is enrolling in a prep course, taking practice exams on your own, or figuring out how best to relax during the exam. If your scores are not particularly high, you can retake the exam. If a second or third try is unsuccessful, it could be useful to explain in your application why the GRE scores do not accurately reflect your potential, but many departments, I suspect, will pay little heed to such explanations.

There is a lot of evidence that test-taking success and test scores are related to family background—social class in particular. Some departments in certain fields that lack diversity provide a little more slack to individuals who come from disadvantaged circumstances. My own view is that departments ought to take more seriously the role of social class in interpreting scores on the GRE, but I would venture to say that this is not common practice in most fields when admission decisions are being made.

Many researchers who study predictors of success in graduate school report that college grades are a robust marker of how students will perform in their PhD program, especially in the early years when students are taking courses. How well they forecast later performance in and after graduate school is another matter altogether. One would expect that college performance might be related to degree completion if only because a student must do well in course work during the early years to get through a program.

If you have a less-than-stellar record as an undergraduate, you had better be prepared to explain why in your personal statement. Admissions committees that take the trouble to look can tell if a difficult start in college affected grade-point average, and they are likely to discount the first year or two if students do very well by the end. The personal statement is also an opportunity to signal experience in a field of study. Admissions committees will often take into account experience such as being a research assistant as an undergraduate, working in a lab, summer employment, and prior papers, particularly if they have resulted in publication. Being explicit about your plans in graduate studies and beyond is a good idea so long as your intentions fit the strengths of a particular department. My department routinely rejects students who want to work in a subspecialty beyond our core strength and accepts students who want to work in a field in which we are strong. That makes sense. So show your stuff, but be aware that what you have to show must fit the strengths and interests of the faculty.

Finally, there is the matter of recommendations from mentors and sponsors. These count, and may count a lot, if the reference is well known and regarded by the faculty. Faculty sponsorship is a critical link in the academic system of training and rewards. Having a strong scholar or, in some programs, a well-regarded practitioner vouch for you can make a huge difference. Generally speaking, letters of recommendation are by their nature full of praise, so only the unique ones stand out.

HOW THE ADMISSIONS PROCESS WORKS

In describing how things generally work in academia, it is important to note that there is almost always some variation in procedures. This is certainly true in admitting graduate students across departments, even in the same discipline. In some cases, particular faculty members decide with whom they will work, particularly if they are able to provide financial support from research grants. In other departments, the entire faculty is involved in the process of choosing students. Some departments have strict weights they apply so that the process is as "objective" as possible. In other departments, an admissions committee evaluates the files and discusses each case at length. Sometimes, the process occurs in two steps: first by a committee and then by the entire faculty. In short, there is no standard operating procedure that regulates selection to a particular program. That is why it makes sense to apply to at least several places.

Ultimately, the final decision of admissions is advisory to the administration or school in which the department resides. However, to my knowledge, graduate admissions rarely are overruled by administrative entities outside the department. Departments are constrained in the amount of money they have to fund graduate students, so typically the administration has either direct or indirect control of the size of the entering cohort. Not surprisingly, the top-ranked departments tend to be better funded and can afford to support many, if not all, students who are admitted. Lesser-ranked and more poorly funded universities often look to students to support themselves for at least part of their graduate studies, placing students in a terrible financial bind.

Self-funding invariably becomes a major cause of dropping out of graduate school. The National Science Foundation recently reported that self-funding of participants in doctoral education has declined significantly over the past decade. Only in the area of doctorates in the field of education does it remain high, but even in this area, self-funding now accounts for slightly less than half of total graduate costs, declining from two-thirds just a decade ago. As the cost of graduate programs rises, self-funding has become unwise for the vast majority of students.[9]

In instances where there are many more applicants than can be accepted, which always happens in the higher-rated departments, the ultimate ranking of incoming students can end up being somewhat arbitrary. There is often an element of gaming involved. Departments want to recruit candidates who will matriculate in their program, so it is not always the most qualified students who are accepted if the reviewers think that such applicants are unlikely to enroll in the program.

Let me explain what often happens. The English department of a large teaching university, which I will call Springmount U, has seven teaching fellowships to award. However, they may lose those fellowships to another department if their designated applicants reject their offer and decide to go elsewhere because they have better options than Springmount. The department's best strategy, then, is to accept the candidates who are most likely to come, even if their credentials are lower than candidates who seem to be headed elsewhere (usually to more highly ranked departments).

It also happens that a given faculty member on the committee is interested in recruiting a certain student because of that student's particular interests, even though the student may not be the strongest applicant in the pool. In other words, the process of admissions to a given program is a little unpredictable. That is why you should apply to a number of appropriate programs. How many? Students, I suspect, have become more risk-averse over time. Just as in the case of college applications, the number of graduate schools to which they apply appears to have increased in my lifetime. I think that it is wise to apply to five to seven universities, which provides ample opportunity to include the top schools and some a bit further down in the rankings, depending on your credentials. Going beyond that number is probably excessive, although I suspect that some readers will not heed this bit of advice.

The more important consideration is what to do if you are admitted to more than one of the schools to which you have applied. I strongly advise you to visit more than one university, meet with faculty with whom you might eventually work, and talk to the graduate students who are in the program. Many departments now stage visiting days for students accepted into the program to meet with students and faculty. The well-heeled universities are often willing to fly students in for a visit and put them up at a nice hotel. Among the principal advantages of visiting are that you get to meet some of your potential peers and compare information and assessments. Just know that the faculty and students are on especially good behavior during these visits, and you may not get a chance to learn about how things will be once you accept. Still, it is a good show, and I highly recommend going if you can.

I always say to potential students, "Faculty will tell you anything you want to hear if they want you to come to the program, but the graduate students will tell you what a program really is like." And what should you ask? Here is a list of concerns that I think warrant consideration in making a good choice among your alternatives.

First, how long does the program typically take to complete? This question is *not* about how long it theoretically could take, but how long it takes most students who enter this particular program. There is an enormous range of expected durations across departments, even within a particular discipline.[10] There are no published guides permitting students to compare the likely length of time that it takes a given cohort to go through graduate programs in a particular discipline, though some of this information can be gleaned from the ratings website of the National Research Council of the National Academy of Sciences. Programs that let students languish in the twilight zone of an almost-completed PhD should get more scrutiny than they often do by unsuspecting applicants. To answer this question, it is necessary for a department or university to have collected the data and make it available to prospective students. A growing number of departments now could make such information available because it is increasingly tracked by the central administration of universities. However, if the statistics are unfavorable, faculty may be disinclined to share the figures with prospective students. You will find that, in fact, many departments do not have this information at hand. If they do not, then *caveat emptor*. At the very least, you should try to get reasonable estimates from the graduate students whom you meet. My advice is not to enter a department if you have little or no idea how long it takes most students to finish their degree and how they finance their time in the program.

Next, find out where the students who completed their degrees in the past five years have been placed. At top-ranked departments, this is not such an issue, but beyond the very top, it is important to know how well the newly minted PhDs are faring. Departments differ in the efforts they make to place their graduates because good placements generally require considerable faculty interest and involvement. You can make a reasonable assessment of where you will be at the end of your training by examining the modal patterns of placement in the various departments to which you have been accepted.

How involved are the faculty in teaching and mentoring students? Some, including the "stars," are no-shows when it comes to offering classes, supervision, and career advice and support. Working closely with faculty, especially in research training and sometimes collaboration, is the essential ingredient of a good graduate education. You must be careful in assuming that you will be able to work with Professor X if you choose his or her department. If training graduate students is not an important part of the departmental culture, you should consider going elsewhere. Important figures in your chosen field may be listed on the roster, but if they are not actively involved in graduate supervision because they are continually on leave, too busy to see students, or merely uninterested in what students can provide to them, you will be frustrated and angry about your graduate training. This means that you must be willing to talk to students about what they are receiving from faculty, how free they feel to initiate contact with members of their faculty, which courses are taught on a regular basis, and so on. In the natural sciences, it is customary to collaborate with faculty; in the social sciences, it is common; and in the humanities, patterns of faculty/student collaboration are more unusual. Still, the amount of faculty training and guidance offered in the program is perhaps the most important criterion for choosing one program over another, given roughly similar rankings.

Departments have distinctly different cultures within the same discipline.[11] Some are much more geared to the students while others are set up more for the benefit of the faculty. Pick a program that has a supportive culture for students. A few good indicators of this are whether faculty work in their offices on a regular basis (as opposed to home or elsewhere), whether students are supported by faculty research projects, whether students and faculty collaborate routinely, whether students complain about exploitation in teaching or research fellowships, the amount that students and faculty talk to one another informally on a regular basis, and how devoted faculty are to placing their graduate students in the job market when they complete the program. In my case, I discovered to my dismay that I had selected a graduate program (at Columbia) that was notoriously indifferent to the interests of the graduate students. Had I spent time talking to some of the graduate students before I entered the program, I might have avoided this fate. Of course, there are always discontented students, but it is pretty easy to decipher the quality of faculty-students relationships if you spend a day or two hanging out.

Another element of department culture is whether graduate students feel they are involved in the intellectual life of the department. Are there regular seminars, are students consulted about elements of the program, are they involved in social events around colloquia and visits by outsiders? Do students get along, study together, enter into collaborations, and support one another? Professional relationships are built and nurtured during graduate school, and it is important that the department facilitate these sorts of bonds. If the graduate students are generally unhappy in a particular program, it is a real danger sign.

FINANCIAL SUPPORT

Financial support is such an important consideration that it deserves its own section. At a private university, graduate tuition alone can run close to $30,000 a year, and the costs go up each year almost as predictably as the changing of the seasons. The top graduate programs at universities with the largest endowments provide much of the support for incoming graduate students. State budgets for public universities are also an important source of graduate support, though in recent years many public universities have been underfunded for graduate programs. Faculty grants also make up another pot of money that supports graduate education.

In many graduate departments and most of the top programs, if you are admitted, you will generally receive at least some financial assistance. I say "generally" because support for graduate training varies by field and by the wealth of the school. However, the entire support package varies greatly nonetheless from program to program. Some schools only support students through their course work and leave it up to them to figure out how to finance the rest by teaching, research jobs, or outside employment. Others require a great deal of teaching in exchange for support. While teaching experience is desirable, too much of it can crowd out course completion, research, and time for writing. In some universities, students are shamelessly exploited as teaching assistants, so it is important to know what obligations you will have for the funding that you receive. As you go down the academic prestige ladder, the support packages are typically less generous.

As might be expected in a highly competitive and presumably meritocratic system, university programs with lesser endowments still compete heavily for the top students, offering inducements such as summer support and small grants in addition to the regular financial package. However, the depth of support offered by a department can have a divisive effect on the students, creating strata of haves and have-nots. Needless to say, this sort of stratification rarely helps the social climate of a department.

Top-quality public institutions provide pretty comparable packages of support, often putting students to work as teaching assistants (TAs) earlier while they are still taking courses. Thus, many graduate students in PhD programs are able to finance their education by gaining teaching and sometimes research experience along the way.[12] However, as I've said, it takes time to be a TA, and it is a daunting task to teach part-time while taking courses, preparing for examinations, conducting research, and writing a dissertation. So even with funding, most graduate students will support themselves by working part-time while taking courses or writing a dissertation. This is not a bad thing, for it is an important part of learning the trade so long as the amount of self-support does not interfere with completing the program in a reasonable number of years. Students can languish in TA or research positions while they try to find time to complete their dissertations.

This situation, which applies even to the most financially secure programs, means that students are working hard and living modestly. Unless you have saved up the money, it might mean taking out loans to make up the difference if you cannot get along on the relatively modest packages of support provided or, as is becoming more common today, cannot count on one's family for financial support. In institutions where the level of support is even more meager, many students will likely have to work full- or part-time to put themselves through graduate school. The trade-offs between moving along swiftly in a PhD program based on loans or lingering much longer by working and going to school can be excruciatingly difficult. A large number of graduate students fail to finish simply because they cannot manage the financial burdens of graduate education.[13] Students, even highly capable ones, may falter in the later years of a graduate program if they get caught in this financial bind.

My advice is to plan financially before you begin graduate school either by saving up, figuring out just how much you can afford to borrow, or by waiting to go to graduate school until you can get the requisite level of support. It can be disastrous to enter graduate school merely with the optimistic hope that it will all work out. Finding out how students support themselves in the department to which you are accepted is essential. If you can anticipate a lengthy spell of part-time graduate school and full-time work in the final years of the program, the likelihood of completing your degree diminishes and the chances of entering a successful academic career are greatly compromised. I'll return to a discussion of the options for slow starters in the next chapter, but for now I will assume that you have financial support in place and are ready to enter graduate school.

A MOMENTOUS TRANSITION

Most first-year graduate students quickly learn that graduate school is not a more concentrated and specialized reprise of undergraduate studies. Graduate training involves a different set of skills, as I have already noted, than what is required to succeed as an undergraduate.[14] While the first two to three years of graduate training are devoted to course work, the courses are designed to equip students with the skills required to practice in the discipline. Graduate school is structured more like an apprenticeship program, aimed at teaching the craft and "the tricks of the trade."[15] To be sure, some of this instruction may be packaged similarly to the material taught to you as an undergraduate, but the aim is for students to use courses as stepping-stones for their own independent research and scholarship.

Students admitted to these programs generally have demonstrated some of these abilities prior to entrance to graduate school. If they don't possess them in advance, they soon learn that they must take the initiative to learn on their own or from more experienced students. Course work provides an introduction to the substantive materials in the field, but it is merely a starting point for a large body of scholarly work, methods and techniques of analysis, and disciplinary practice.

Expect to work extremely hard in graduate school. Between classes, teaching or research assistantships, studying for exams, and writing papers, it sometimes seems impossible to get everything done—good preparation for an academic career. I haven't conducted an official survey, but graduate students put in long hours for little remuneration. While they may complain about the workload, most understand the point of it. There is so much to learn, and the early years seem to pass quickly, at least in retrospect. Lest I make the experience sound blissful, for most it is hardly that. It is more like running a marathon—a great challenge that requires discipline, training, and stamina.[16]

First-year students often feel intimidated by the high expectations, the work demands, the need to juggle many demanding tasks, and, not least of all, by both their fellow students and the faculty. Entering students, after a week or two of classes, sometimes confide to me that they are not as prepared, well read, practiced in methods, smart as other students, and the list goes on and on. I certainly had these fears when I entered graduate school. Such invidious comparisons and self-doubts are common in the first year when students observe that their peers know things they do not, arrive with training or experience that they have not received, or seem to understand classes and assignments faster than they do.

Of course, there is a paradox in these perceptions: how could everyone find that their fellow students are smarter and better trained than they? This illusion is a by-product of the recognition of how much there is to learn. Students are acutely aware of how much they don't know, ignoring or taking for granted what they do. Generally speaking, programs, especially the more select ones, do not admit students who cannot do the work or complete a degree. There are exceptions, however. Some departments admit large cohorts and subscribe to the precept of sink or swim. Many students exit with a master's degree, leaving behind the most persistent and, perhaps, the most promising to proceed in the PhD program. Think carefully before you enter such a program because it is a cruel way to manage the selection process and often produces a dog-eat-dog environment, especially during the critical early years.

Nonetheless, there is an inevitable sorting that takes place in the course of graduate education, and this sorting begins almost immediately, though faculty are rarely able to get a very good fix on a given student's prospects from a single course or even their performance in the first year of the program. Some students take to graduate school like a duck to water while for others the initial years may be bumpy. The sorting process that occurs in the early years is fluid as slow starters begin to gain skills and initial hotshots sometimes falter. In other words, do not panic if your initial entry into graduate school is inauspicious. If you are enjoying your first year, at least by the end, it is a good sign.

By your second year, you will have a good sense of how you are faring. Many students entering graduate school have become accustomed to being highly regarded academic prospects. It is never easy discovering that you have entered a whole world of highly regarded prospects.

RELATIONS WITH FACULTY

Dealings with faculty can be quite overwhelming in the initial stages of graduate school. Scholars whose work you studied as an undergraduate, brilliant professors who are showing their stuff, hard-assed sergeants committed to making your life miserable by exposing your ignorance or follies—they come in all sizes and shapes. Of course, there are nice folks, too, who appear human and who take a keen interest in the welfare of their students. One of the most important parts of your training is being able to work with difficult faculty (assuming that they have important things to teach you) and using supportive faculty well and wisely.

There is a good deal of leeway in academia, at least compared with other professions, to—let's put it delicately—be your own person. So characters who might be fired in other lines of work abound and even thrive in academic life. Eccentricities, self-centeredness, or even downright ornery behavior is more tolerated than might be otherwise in less insulated organizations. These sorts of negative traits may be offset by qualities such as originality, intellectual breadth, and outright brilliance. Of course, it is also possible that difficult people have little to offer. You must decide for yourself.

My advisor and principal mentor in graduate school, William J. Goode, was a notoriously difficult character, and he worked with relatively few students during his illustrious academic career. I am indebted to him because he taught me how to think as a sociologist, but I can't say that dealing with him was one of the pleasures of my time in grad school. In most departments, whatever the discipline, there are at least one or two people like him who thrive on their critical sensibilities. Don't always be put off by difficult faculty. You will encounter plenty of them along the way. Just figure out, as best you can, how to work with them if they have something to offer to you. One simply does not have the luxury of telling them what you think of their style—at least not yet!

At the other end of the continuum are faculty whom you love for their kindness, commitment, and concern. Again, they come in all forms: some who have a lot to teach you and others who are perhaps kind but not really that helpful to your intellectual development. You must be able to sort out the people whom you like and the people who deserve your respect and attention, even if you don't particularly care for them, so long as they are ethical and not too abusive or crazy.

You can learn a lot through word of mouth. Faculty whom you respect can sometimes give you signals about their colleagues, although there is a general norm, occasionally only observed in the breach, that faculty members do not reveal to students their colleagues' limitations. Therefore, the signals from advisors and mentors may be subtle, especially in the early years of graduate school when your ties with faculty are just forming. Senior graduate students are perhaps more reliable informants about what different faculty might have to offer, but again take some care in relying too completely on one or two students for such information. Mostly, it's up to you to figure out how much you can learn and benefit from working with members of your faculty.

Regardless of personal style, it is generally crucial to acquire a good mentor or two, preferably in the early years of your program. Mentors serve as intellectual role models, as coaches who train and monitor your work, and later as sponsors who connect you to the outside scholarly world. It is difficult to manage the early part of your career well without a "case manager." As I've said, graduate programs are like an apprenticeship, admitting people into the guild. While exams and research test your knowledge and skills, ultimately the masters/mistresses of the guild hold the keys to admittance into their ranks. They get to decide the rules, judge your progress, and determine when you are ready to be awarded your PhD.

This all sounds very paternal/maternalistic, but there are various checks in place to keep faculty from abusing their powers. Nonetheless, I cannot say that abuse of power never occurs. It does happen, and it happens more in some departments than in others. Faculty can be irresponsible about grading exams and papers. One illustrious member of my graduate faculty was notorious for holding up dissertations by never finding time to read drafts of students' theses, and a few of my peers, some very talented, lingered in a continual state of purgatory.

It should be apparent by now that getting to know faculty well in the early years of your training, during the course work and preliminary exams, is essential, particularly in preparing to organize a dissertation committee. The good news is that well-functioning departments afford many such opportunities to get to know faculty members on a formal and informal basis. Many have regular colloquia where visiting scholars, members of the faculty, or students present papers or give talks. These occasions provide you with an opportunity to observe how members of the faculty behave in semi-public situations. Periodically, most departments have informal mixers or celebrations. Don't be shy about attending these occasions. True, they take time away from your studies, but they provide occasions to explore interests in common, job possibilities, and catch up on professional gossip. It is important to reach out and take the initiative to deepen your relationships with faculty and other graduate students.

My department has an annual meeting of the faculty to discuss all of the first- and second-year students. Although the number of the students in our program is relatively small, it occasionally happens that no one can say much about a particular student. The faculty regards this as a serious shortcoming. We consider it failure on our part, but we also regard it as a failure on the part of the student, who has shown too little initiative in the early years of the program. Students who are culturally predisposed to keeping too much social distance, preternaturally shy, or given to social isolation are a concern to us because these traits can pose problems for their academic success in building the necessary relationships to get through the program.

ORGANIZING YOUR TIME

Too much to do and too little time is a chronic complaint among graduate students in all disciplines. The feeling of being overloaded with obligations is omnipresent, and with good reason, so managing time and the accompanying stress of working long hours is imperative in graduate school. I offer some tips in this regard.

Once you get the lay of the land in your department, figure out a regular work schedule. Developing routines for work and for those things that bolster your emotional survival are essential. The most successful graduate students are typically those who know how to manage and keep control of their schedules. The common undergraduate practice of putting off assignments until the last minute can be imminent death in graduate school. Dashing off papers at the last minute simply won't work well unless you are the type of person who can write an excellent first draft. Few students, or faculty for that matter, can pull off a feat like this on a regular basis. Besides, it gets harder and harder over time to endure those all-nighters. Once in a while perhaps, but I know very few successful academics who do all-nighters often or even ever.

Managing multiple tasks at once is extremely difficult, and young scholars must develop a good sense of how to set priorities and when to call it quits on an assignment. It is important to be able to maintain your stamina for work over weeks and months at a time. There are times when your course work becomes all consuming, but sustaining your commitment requires slack periods as well when you can put your energies elsewhere by going to the gym, socializing, or attending movies or a concert. However, it is hard to be completely spontaneous in seeking these needed sources of relaxation; you are better off planning for them by building them into your schedule. And even so, there will be many occasions when they will be abandoned for lack of time.

Once you learn the regular milestones of your particular program (completing course work, qualifying exams, and, of course, thesis proposal and doctoral defense), then you can develop a timetable for completing them. Some departments such as mine put a lot of pressure on students to adhere to a schedule outlining each milestone, as we firmly believe that students do better under these structured conditions. Others feel that it is up to students to set their own pace and are relatively laissez-faire in the timing of the milestones. When the rules are clear, students tend to move relatively quickly, as the peer norms tend to operate to keep everyone on schedule. Lacking such a timetable, there tends to be more slippage and hence fewer pressures to stay on schedule.

GRADUATE STUDENT CULTURES

Academic relationships that begin in graduate school often survive for a lifetime. No matter how well managed a graduate program is, students are in a stressful environment and often develop strong bonds as a result.[17] Not quite foxhole buddies, but something like that. Besides, students find that it is useful if not essential to collaborate. Whether studying for exams, teaching one another in the lab, reading each others' papers or dissertation proposals, or forming a dissertation reading group, it makes sense to work together. Earlier in this chapter, I stressed the importance of being able to work on your own. However, collaboration is required in many disciplines and welcomed in many others. The lone scholar at work is probably a more accurate picture of what occurs in the humanities; it is far less applicable in most social and natural sciences. Academics need to exchange information, teach one another, and work together on projects, and those skills are cultivated in graduate school.

While a great deal is written on the subcultures of high schools and colleges, relatively little research has been carried out on this topic in graduate education. Qualities such as competition or collaboration, disunity or cohesion, alienation or loyalty will vary among departments in any given discipline. I spoke of it earlier when talking about selecting among departments when you enter graduate school. And within departments, friction sometimes arises between students along ideological lines (clinical vs. non-clinical, theoretical vs. empirical, qualitative vs. quantitative, and so on) that may reflect differences among the faculty. These cultures are partially a reflection of faculty relations. A well-known sociological study on mental hospitals found that when the professional staff does not get along, the patients are more likely to express symptoms of distress.[18] It may not be quite that bad, but something like that surely occurs within graduate school departments.

Academics have a notorious reputation for their inability to get along within departments. Graduate students can get caught up in rivalries or professional debates all too easily. While intellectually these differences can be stimulating and thought provoking, they can also bog you down in fruitless conflict. Years ago my department, like many others in my field, experienced tensions between qualitative and quantitative research approaches, which often played out in student cleavages. Over time, I am happy to say that these differences melted away as more and more of us began to integrate both modes of data collection in our research. Now students in our department with somewhat different research proclivities team together or set out to become skilled in both techniques of data collection and analysis. The cultural split in the department has all but disappeared, and I dare say that students are happier for the change.

Dangers in the opposite direction exist as well. Choosing a given department where all faculty members subscribe to a particular disciplinary viewpoint can create headaches if you seek jobs in departments that may not hold these views. Although this is less likely to happen in the natural sciences than in the humanities or social sciences, it surely occurs in all fields and can have an insidious effect on students who become loyal advocates of a particular disciplinary point of view. Economists who are trained to be skeptical of the wisdom of free markets, for example, may be dismissed out of hand during their job search by a department that does not hold these views.[19] Selection of a graduate program may instill certain beliefs and practices that can be reinforced by exposure to a graduate student culture that limits rather than expands the scope of legitimate intellectual inquiry.

DISCIPLINARY IDEOLOGY

Academic divisions can be especially insidious when intellectual differences become overlaid with ideological considerations that extend beyond the discipline. This is particularly true of, although hardly restricted to, the humanities and social sciences, in which ideological debates are laced with political and cultural criticism and where the scholarly and scientific work can be difficult to separate from personal views associated with religion, politics, gender, race, and a host of other distinctions.

In sociology, these ideologies intrude in countless explicit and implicit ways that influence choice of research topics and data analysis and interpretation. I like to think, even if it isn't always true, that academic disciplines provide a number of checks and balances for managing the potentially intrusive role of ideology. You must learn to take seriously the methods of the discipline if you are to be open to uncomfortable and unfamiliar views. In the natural sciences, this may be less of a problem, but in the social sciences and humanities, it is a critical challenge for younger scholars not to put on intellectual blinders as they move through graduate training.

When I was a graduate student, work linking sociological and biological bases of behavior was regarded with extreme suspicion. After World War II, social science became very wary of rooting social behavior in biological origins. Recent advances in genetics, physiology, and neuroscience have given rise to new interchanges between biological, psychological, and social behavior that make it compelling to cross fields to understand how multiple influences on human behavior operate in tandem. Nonetheless, I still find that many senior scholars who were trained decades ago resist, largely for ideological reasons, the enterprise of examining the biological roots of social behavior and the impact of social contexts on human development.

Graduate students (and young faculty) can face problems when they attempt to cross disciplinary boundaries because disciplines jealously guard their intellectual turf. I will say more about these challenges later on, but it is important to recognize that disciplines do have their boundaries. How often have I heard a colleague say to a student, "Why is that a sociological problem? I can see why a psychologist might be interested in what you are doing, but why is it a sociological issue?" That is not an unreasonable question; this concern is inevitably raised when fields are being breached. You need to know that boundary crossing can be hazardous to do while in graduate school, although some programs are designed to welcome or even promote endeavors to build bridges between disciplines, such as communications, neuroscience, or ethnohistory. Not infrequently, students are encouraged or required to take courses outside their discipline, but when it comes to writing a dissertation proposal, interdisciplinary work may be subtly discouraged.

My advice: Be brave but be wise in your willingness to cross the disciplines, and be prepared to make a strong case for what you are doing. Intellectual fashions change as old truths are discarded for new ones. You may be ahead of your time, but it is absolutely essential to realize that when you cross disciplinary boundaries as a graduate student, someone is likely to raise an eyebrow. Disciplines are inherently conservative, even though what they conserve is constantly changing.

There is a distinct sequence of stages to graduate school that come with different rhythms and routines. Students experience an understandable sense of accomplishment as they complete their courses, pass specialty exams or prelims, and craft a dissertation project. Many programs require that you complete a master's degree before you are officially permitted to enter the PhD program. This staging occurs in part to weed out students who are not well qualified or are poorly suited to go on, and, as such, this hurdle in many departments represents a point of decision both for faculty and the students.

This is also a normal point when students who feel they have made a poor choice, either in their plans to attain a PhD or in the university or department, can alter their course. Some switch to other programs; it is a relatively easy time to transfer because many departments will give full or partial credit for a master's degree earned elsewhere. It is also possible to switch to a different PhD program. Many departments admit students from other institutions if they have performed well. The completion of a master's degree is sometimes a good opportunity to move up the academic ladder by switching to a better-ranked program or one that offers substantive specialties closer to your interests.

For students whose doubts about the wisdom of getting a PhD have grown during the early years of course work, it is a time to think hard about whether it is sensible to continue. Depending on the field, a master's degree can provide a credential for employment in the private sector, nonprofits, or high-end secondary education. For students who may be beset by doubts about whether it makes sense to go on, it is the best time to leave a graduate program with some dignity, and perhaps finances, intact while retaining the possibility of returning later with a renewed sense of purpose or commitment. Students facing the prospect of leaving graduate school may want to consult the following chapter, which discusses non-academic careers.

If you are proceeding beyond the master's degree, you should by now have a clear sense of where you are headed in your education. In all likelihood, at this point at the end of the second or third year of your program, you do not yet have a dissertation topic. However, you should be in the early stages of choosing a topic, selecting one or more mentors, and preparing for prelims or area exams. These are the markers that map progress through the later years of your graduate studies.

Almost all graduate programs require some form of pre-doctoral examinations, although examination procedures come in a variety of packages. Oral exams, written prelims or area specialties, prelim papers, and various combinations of each of these may be required in your program during or after the third or fourth year of a program. You should have a clear idea of how the exam system operates and what is specifically required in the way of preparation long before the time you take comprehensive or special area examination. Depending on the discipline and the exam procedure, students often study for several months before they take their PhD exams. You can get a running start on your preparation in the early years by keeping good reading notes, identifying essential readings that must be completed for your exams, and, most of all, gaining a clear understanding of the types of questions that are posed in the exams. I am always amazed at how few students have looked at previous prelims or discussed them in detail with fellow students who have already taken them before they begin studying for their examinations. Gaining a sense of what you will need to know early on in your graduate career can help a lot in organizing your preparation for prelims.

I tell my students to view these exams as an opportunity to read and learn a body of literature, to think deeply about a set of issues central to your field of study, and to identify interesting areas of future work that may eventually end up in your dissertation. Decades later I am still surprised by how much I read and how much I remember of what I read. My file of three-by-five cards (now it would be a computer file) grew steadily during my graduate career to several file boxes by the time of my exams (a two-hour oral exam).

It is a formative period, and something akin to imprinting occurs in an exam preparation that often lasts for a long time. Of course, that is a highly idealized picture of examinations; it is hard for students to feel that way when they are going through the process of being tested, often by close and respected mentors or sometimes by faculty rogues who may slip in a tricky question.

I suspect that a relatively high proportion of students get through the exam stage, but, as far as I know, there are no statistics on how many students falter at this point. In my own department, it is infrequent for students to fail MA prelims or PhD area examinations. This does not lower the level of anxiety among the students as much as you would expect, however. The ritual itself is sufficiently powerful that students study diligently and still feel that their standing in the department, if not their career, is on the line.

One effective way of studying for exams and perhaps of managing some of the accompanying anxiety is to form a study group with other students. There is real efficiency in reading and studying together that offers the added dividends of discussing and understanding information and knowledge about relevant topics, debates, unsettled issues and questions. Exams typically test knowledge and analytic ability. Ongoing discussions with peers can strengthen both. In addition, it helps to gauge your level of preparation by these sorts of group exchanges.

An important transformation takes place as students go through the prelim process, as it frequently involves a growing level of specialization within a discipline. Students are generally required to concentrate on one or more select areas within the broader corpus of their discipline. This process of specialization produces a professional identity, which is likely to last throughout your academic career. Moving through graduate school, you emerge as a labor historian, an expert on late nineteenth-century French literature, or a neuroscientist with interests in cognitive development. These specializations or subfields within a discipline typically align with how many departments divide their academic turf. Usually, these special areas are commonly understood in a given discipline. However, if they are not recognized, you had better be well prepared to explain your identity to others in your field.

Your scholarly identity crystallizes further in selecting a dissertation topic. Many, probably the vast majority, of academics end up working in the subspecialty of their doctoral topic throughout much, if not all, of their academic career. This happens quite naturally and sometimes unconsciously in the course of graduate school as you discover your intellectual tastes, acquire academic sponsorship, and begin working on research projects. As you begin to form a professional identity, you will be accumulating intellectual and social capital that serves you well in your search for a job later on. Therefore specialization in graduate school is something that you should manage carefully, if only because it takes some time and effort to change your professional identity later on. The point is to make this decision deliberately and with your eyes open to the constraints that it may introduce later on.

Dissertation topics are conceived in a variety of ways. A good deal of your course work and interaction with faculty and fellow students is devoted to learning what you need to know in order to ask an interesting research question in your discipline. Some students have already decided what they want to do by the time they arrive in graduate school, although not infrequently such declarations dissolve in the early years of course work. For others—and this occurs far more often in the natural and behavioral sciences—the choice of a topic comes through working with a mentor who essentially assigns or recommends a thesis topic that is closely related to his or her research agenda. The very idea that a dissertation topic is assigned to a student is an anathema to many fields in the humanities. We social scientists certainly encourage students to work on topics that we think are important, but just as often students approach us with a topic and we help them to shape it into a manageable project.

There is no shortage of lore and advice for how to select a dissertation topic. I've heard of faculty telling their students not to work on anything that they care too deeply about, and just as often others advise students to follow their passions. My take on this advice leans toward the latter viewpoint, but not everyone can or will fall in love with their dissertation topic. It is entirely possible to think of it more like cohabitation than marriage—something that seems to be promising and appealing but that you could outgrow in the course of time.

Although fields vary somewhat on the premium placed on originality, in my discipline students typically design projects that speak to questions that are unsettled or in play. Students are expected to build on a scholarly tradition rather than fashion a question that is detached from an existing body of work. Or, at the very least, they must locate their question in a body of theory and prior work that makes the question appear inevitably important for their colleagues to care about the answer. "Why should I care about this research question?" is one of the most devastating remarks that can be made at a dissertation proposal defense. By the time you get to your defense, the justification for your topic should be obvious and compelling, and you should certainly be prepared to make it so if such questions arise.

A doctoral thesis must be achievable within a reasonable time frame. A common dilemma among graduate students is to propose doing far more than is possible to accomplish—a recipe for frustration if not disaster. A far too ambitious scope of work can lead students to do too much work with not enough depth or to undertake a study that will simply take too long to complete in a reasonable length of time. A year to two years is fairly standard in most fields, though some disciplines that involve fieldwork can require a longer time commitment. The opposite of working on a topic that is too slight or insignificant is probably less precarious in the short run, but it may leave little at the end of publishable quality. You are striving to adhere to the Goldilocks principle: just the right amount of work that launches you into an area that leads to some logical next steps. Your dissertation is best thought of as a down payment on a longer-term commitment to a more ambitious future agenda of research.

Part of managing your graduate career well is building toward your dissertation proposal during your course work and examinations. Too many students put off the question of a thesis topic until they complete their course work and even after their prelims. You can establish a good intellectual foundation for your professional identity by thinking of your graduate work as cumulative, defining and directing your topic by the selections of courses and possibly (depending on your field and department) your choice of examination areas. Wandering in the delights of different areas is a good way to start, but by the time you are in your third or fourth year of graduate school, it is time to impose some direction to your interests. Although it is not necessarily true to say that the sooner you start doing this, the better, it is true that if you don't start early enough, it will add years to your graduate studies, which ultimately can become a problem for you on the job market.

COMPLETING THE DISSERTATION

As I've indicated, different fields as well as departments within disciplines have an implicit, if not an explicit, timetable for completing the dissertation.[20] A recent study by the Council of Graduate Schools found that slightly more than half of the students in two recent PhD cohorts completed their doctoral thesis within ten years.[21] Of course, the dropouts from graduate school are included in the half that did not complete their dissertation. Probably relatively few of those not finishing in ten years will ever complete their thesis. That figure of one-half is actually somewhat higher than previous studies have indicated. However, the sample of schools included was restricted and somewhat biased toward higher completion rates.[22]

Across (and even within) disciplines, the variation in both timing and attrition is sizable. Completion rates are highest among scientists and engineers and lowest among the humanities, with the social sciences falling in the middle. Successful students indicated the importance of financial support, mentoring, family support (presumably both economic and psychological assistance), and advice garnered from professional sources. Indeed, an important determinant of the length of graduate school is the financial requirement of supporting yourself in the latter years. Only the elite and wealthy institutions, as I noted earlier, provide sufficient funding to sustain students from beginning to end. No doubt, the financial aid provided to engineering and natural sciences greatly contributes to the higher completion rates provided by these fields.

Apart from the prominent role that financial support plays in completion, differences in requirements and guidance affect the rate of attrition and the length required to complete a PhD. Anthropologists rarely finish in less than seven years while economists often do. This may have to do with mastering different bodies of knowledge, but just as often the timetable is permitted much more flexibility and individual discretion in some fields and departments than others. Clearly, when work requires learning new languages, archival research requiring permissions and other hurdles, or going out into the field to collect data, it simply takes longer than might be the case when using existing data sets or working in labs that provide many of the building blocks for your project. However, you do have some control over the time it will take by your choice of department, mentor, and the amount of self-direction you are able to impose upon yourself.

A good deal of the attrition occurs in the latter phases of the PhD program, particularly in the final stage of completing a dissertation. This is when financial support declines, loans begin to accumulate, and outside jobs may crowd out time for research and writing. Not coincidentally, it is also the point at which guidance from mentors can flag if students lose contact with their advisors. Generally speaking, it becomes difficult for students who must work outside the department to retain regular contact with and support from their advisors.

There are some useful strategies for students who want to avoid disappearing out of sight while writing their dissertation. First and foremost, it is essential to maintain contact with your mentors and advisors even when you are off-site. As I said at the outset of this chapter, your choice of a mentor is probably the most critical decision that you will make in graduate school. She or he is the person who provides a lifeline during the latter stages of your graduate career, including during the writing phase. It is this stage where too many students hit a brick wall. Students whose progress on their dissertation stalls are often hesitant to contact their advisors, and advisors are not always as conscientious as they might be about staying in touch with their wayward students, owing to the pressures of teaching, research, and departmental responsibilities. "It is the student's responsibility to get in touch with me" is, no doubt, a common sentiment of dissertation advisors. In recent years, the pressure has grown among departments to do a better job of monitoring students in the dissertation writing stage, but progress on this front has been slower than it should be.

What can you do if your advisor doesn't respond to your requests for assistance or, worse yet, does not read a draft of your thesis in a reasonably timely fashion? Persist. When faculty advisors disappear, they must be held to account; or if they cannot be, you must take the difficult step of trying to replace them with a more responsive advisor. Understandably, students are reluctant to pressure their advisors because they are their principal links to the job world. However, it behooves you to not let long lapses in communication occur because doing so can undermine your motivation to forge on with research and writing. Having invested a number of years in a graduate program, take the initiative to get the necessary help, even if asking for help feels uncomfortable. While I am not advocating the general principle of being a squeaky wheel in graduate school, you cannot accept an advisor who stonewalls your efforts to get an appointment or to have your dissertation drafts read at this critical point in your graduate career. It is unfair and it is unprofessional.

Seeing a dissertation to the end also requires that you establish a clear and realistic timetable for writing. This, of course, is frequently a topic of discussion in a dissertation proposal and a proposal defense, but frequently the timetable proves to be too ambitious. If that is the case, you and your advisor must renegotiate your scope of work (if it is too large) or your schedule (if it cannot be maintained).

How to keep on track in writing a dissertation is the most critical challenge that most graduate students face in the course of their studies. There are some simple tips for maintaining your schedule: Try to devote a fixed number of hours each week to your dissertation. This is very hard for students who have jobs, families, and obligations beyond graduate school, but it is critical to finishing. Spending as little as two to four hours every day is far better than cramming all your writing in over one month during the summer; it takes more time to start up from a dead stop that may have by then lasted several months. Data analysis and especially writing are very much like exercise. If you do it regularly, it is not too painful.

I will say more about writing in later chapters, but I firmly believe that, especially in the early years of academic life, you must acquire a set of habits that work for you. Finding a time and place to write is a critical one. I like to write first thing in the morning because I function better early in the day, but it might be just the opposite for you. What matters is that you develop a set of routines that suit your work style.

Try to write something every working day, even if you think that you don't have much to say. Writing is a habit, and you will find that it becomes far easier to do if you have a routine. Don't censor yourself as you are writing. Students generally are their own worst critics, and it is almost impossible to write if you are criticizing yourself as you go along. You will have plenty of opportunities to exercise your critical capacities when you edit and revise.

Show your early drafts to peers; they'll provide the support and helpful comments you need before you submit your work to your advisor. If they don't understand what you are trying to say, discussing the content and ideas with them will help clarify your writing. I strongly advise participating in a dissertation group in which students present their work to one another. This can be helpful in the proposal writing stage, but it becomes even more important when you begin to write your thesis. Dissertation groups can cut down on the feeling of intellectual and social isolation that sometimes occurs toward the end of a graduate career.

Assuming that you have your drafts in a reasonable form, show them to your principal advisor sooner rather than later. Early feedback is essential. It may be painful to expose yourself to criticism, but it is a necessary step along the way to getting it right. Besides, it is a lifelong requirement of being an academic.

Don't feel you must begin writing at chapter 1. It sometimes is easier to write the substantive chapters containing your methods, data analysis, and interpretive materials than to frame the thesis from the start. Presumably, some of the framing has been done in your proposal, but you may find that it is necessary to reframe your analysis and can do so only after it has been completed. Some students benefit from writing memos describing their findings before they organize them into chapters.

Don't be too hard on yourself. Most students I know enter a fog-like period when they start putting their dissertations together. They sometimes feel like they are wandering without a clear path of direction in describing their findings. A clear sense of direction may only occur by trial and error or from comments from early readers. Most students get better at writing up their results as they go along and begin to see how to put their ideas and findings together into a coherent package.

Your dissertation is to some extent an academic exercise and to some extent a professional piece of work. Understand the differences between the two. Your faculty readers may be looking for much more detail in your theoretical framing, review of relevant literature, analytic methods, findings, and interpretation than would be acceptable in publication. To the extent that you can put some of this material in appendices in your dissertation, you will not have to remove it later when you turn your thesis into articles or a book.

In some fields, including my own, it is now acceptable to write several articles that are loosely connected with an overview and conclusion. In fields where papers are more valued than books, this approach can make a lot of sense. Essentially, students are permitted to write three publishable articles instead of a book-like thesis. This has the distinct advantage of bringing the work closer to publication. Clearly, this style is inappropriate in fields where books are the coin of the realm.

THE DISSERTATION DEFENSE

The dissertation defense in most fields is a mixture of examination, rite of passage, and ceremonial occasion blended differently depending on the discipline and the norms of the department. In some locales, and commonly in European universities, students are expected to present a lecture after which they field questions from their examiners and the audience. In other cases, it is a private affair between the student and examining committee. Committees are typically formed before a thesis proposal is written, but members may be added from outside the department on the occasion of the defense. If not required to present their findings in a formal lecture, candidates are typically asked to briefly summarize their important findings for the committee, which presumably has already carefully read the dissertation. This gives the event a certain solemnity, turning the PhD candidate into teacher—expressing the symbolic admittance into the professoriate.

The defense is the culmination of the graduate student career, a licensing examination with the outcome generally predetermined by the examiners. I say predetermined because it is rare for a dissertation defense to end in failure. It happens, to be sure, but a good committee will not generally let the graduate student defend a dissertation that is seriously flawed. By the point of the examination, the readers in most fields and most departments do not let the defense occur unless they have reason to believe it will be successful.

In my discipline as in many, the chair of the committee orchestrates the process. He or she has read and critiqued previous drafts and often consults with the other readers prior to the examination. If there are serious reservations, efforts are made to provide feedback in advance of the exam so that the student can make revisions and attempt to satisfy potential criticisms. If the dissertation defense goes poorly, it reflects badly not only on the student but also on the chair of the committee.

So a prudent chair assumes responsibility for making sure that his or her colleagues have their say before the defense is scheduled.

That planning, even though the student is often involved in and aware of the process, hardly dampens the uncertainty and anxiety associated with the actual defense. No matter how poised and prepared students are by the time of the event, it is rare for them not to be awed by the significance of it. That is how it is meant to be because the PhD defense is the final licensing examination and thus a transformative experience for graduate students when they emerge from the examination room as PhDs.

Of course, it is often not quite that simple. Frequently a student is passed with the expectation that there will be further revisions before the dissertation is filed. Under some circumstances, the passing student will be required to get approval from one or more members of the committee before he or she is permitted to file the thesis, a procedure required for administrative purposes in order to receive the PhD at graduation. Such revisions may be minor or they can be fairly substantial. In rare instances, the work may be substantial enough to require a reexamination or a postponed graduation date.

When it works well, the dissertation defense can be exhilarating whether it takes the form of a lecture or an extended conversation between the student and an animated examination committee. In that sense, it is a powerful rite of passage, admitting the student into the academic guild. I must confess that the power of the occasion still lingers with me four decades later. From time to time, I still dream about being in my defense, often wondering why I am still being examined when I already have a PhD!

Preparing for a defense involves being able to describe the importance of your work in a succinct manner, understanding its strengths and limitations, and anticipating criticisms in advance. Remember that in all likelihood, you will be the greatest authority on your own piece of research, knowing more about its flaws than your committee. That does not require you to dwell on the problems, nor does it mean that you should ignore them altogether. Appropriate demeanor at the defense can be viewed as a model for how one responds to academic criticism more generally, sorting out the comments that demand a stout response and those that require acknowledgment of weaknesses or limitations that require repair or, perhaps more often, future investigation.

Believe it or not, the graduate career for many often goes more swiftly than they can imagine. Five, seven, or even ten years later, you are the recipient of a PhD, having survived what is almost invariably a demanding if not grueling process, culminating in your PhD examination. Now what? The commencement is over, but you are just beginning the journey in your academic career. In the following chapter, I consider your options for the next step.

2

AN ACADEMIC CAREER OR NOT?

Long before you complete your PhD or its professional equivalent, you already know that you will be facing an important fork in the road: whether to seek an academic or non-academic job. For some readers, this "choice" may be more apparent than real. The labor market and the availability of academic positions could make the decision for you. In a growing number of academic specialties, especially in the humanities, there has long been a significant gap between the number of PhDs in any given field—far greater for some disciplines than others—and the number of academic job openings each year. It is no secret to anyone reading this book that this gap has increased over the past decade in an alarming fashion in certain fields such as history, modern languages, and philosophy, to mention some conspicuous examples.[1]

As you know by now, this guide is designed primarily for readers who are heading for an academic job. But in fields such as public policy, education, health, and many disciplines in the sciences and engineering, an academic job that is primarily devoted to teaching is not the objective of going to graduate school or of getting an advanced degree. Academics generally like their jobs and are inclined to believe that all students capable of an academic career should pursue one. However, the vast majority of PhD recipients do not end up as full-time academics. For many if not most, a career in a university or college was never part of their plans. Others who thought they might like to teach full-time when they entered a graduate program discover that they lack the taste or the right skill set for the academic world. But many readers are still weighing their options as they finish their doctorate. This chapter may be especially useful to those who have not made up their minds about whether to pursue an academic career or not.

A former graduate student of mine—I'll call her Rachel Neely—told me about an encounter she had with one of my colleagues her first day at Penn. "He asked me why I had decided to enter the graduate program. I told him that I was interested in health policy. His face dropped instantly and he said to me, 'If you aren't interested in an academic career, you came to the wrong place.'" My colleague was expressing an attitude all too common among social scientists that it is a waste of time to train people who are not headed for a university position, or at least one at a good teaching college. I should add that Rachel did brilliantly in the program and ended up taking an academic position after finishing her PhD. However, after a few years of teaching, she found that she was growing increasingly impatient with many of the fruitless meetings and committees that crowded out her research agenda and distracted from her teaching. One day she confessed to me—fearful that I would disapprove of her decision—that she decided to follow her initial passion and accept a research job. I can happily report that Rachel is now doing important and creative work. Although she does not preclude the possibility of returning to teaching and academic research later in life, she does not feel impelled to do so. The lesson is, of course, that not everyone is suited to academia even when they are well qualified for a teaching position.

THE ATTRACTIONS OF A CAREER OUTSIDE OF ACADEMIA

Although I will have much less to say about non-academic careers beyond this chapter, readers should not assume that I personally subscribe to the view that an academic career is the best choice that you can make with a PhD. My own research program brings me into frequent contact with policymakers, researchers in think tanks and public- and private-sector organizations, clinicians, and program administrators, many of whom have doctorates in economics, psychology, sociology, demography, and education, to mention only some of the disciplines in which non-academic jobs for PhDs abound. When it comes to intelligence, creativity, productivity, and all the other qualities that professors generally value, I find little to distinguish my colleagues inside and outside of academia. I suspect the same is true in the biological and physical sciences and engineering, where most jobs for PhDs are outside of academia.

The challenges and demands of non-academic jobs are different, but they are no less onerous. True, many academics wrinkle up their noses at non-academics and vice versa, but the intellectual and professional worlds overlap to a high degree. There are good reasons for selecting one path rather than another, but my advice is to follow your passions, your talents, and your predispositions, assuming you have a choice in the matter. This book is designed to help you decide whether you want to be an academic and how best to achieve this objective. I include some tips for those who are planning to work outside of a traditional professorial career so that readers who could go either way might give more serious consideration to working outside of academia.

So let me begin by giving some of the reasons *not* to be an academic and what may be appealing about using your PhD outside the confines of the ivory tower. Graduate programs in many disciplines are beginning to realize, too, that they may want to emphasize and train students for non-academic jobs; for example, in history the discipline is beginning to think about how to expand the graduate curriculum to prepare students for non-academic positions.[2] The vignette about Rachel hints at some good reasons for preferring a non-academic job. Academics, especially in the traditional disciplines of arts and sciences, are not typically movers and shakers in society, industry, or government. If you want to change the world, there may be good reasons for getting a doctorate, but an academic job is not necessarily the ideal place for you. You will have to do a number of things that distract you from effecting social change, helping others, or making a difference in the world. Sure, there are plenty of exceptions to this rule, but most academics I know are—let's put it delicately—pretty academic people. Most are not that interested in the nitty-gritty of institutional change, the nuts and bolts of making organizations effectively accomplish their missions, or the practicalities of getting something accomplished—unless it happens to be the topic of their own field of research. Academics tend to have an unusual taste for ideas, a tolerance for the abstract, and a belief—

sometimes self-delusional—that what we are working on is important, even when others find it difficult to understand why. I hate to say it, but most people are not like academics!

If you are one of those people like Rachel who finds academic life too insular, precious, and unreal, you probably should consider a non-academic job. If endless talk about ideas and abstractions bores you to death, academic life is probably not for you. If you like tasks that you can complete in a discrete amount of time, you may not thrive in academia, where work often cannot be readily accomplished in fixed chunks of time. If you crave the gratifications of service, helping others, and teamwork, I'm not sure that academic life provides the best setting to fulfill these objectives. Sure, I can think of activities that provide outlets in my job enabling me to fulfill those needs, but they are generally not well rewarded, especially in higher-ranking academic settings.

There are, of course, positions in academia that afford greater latitude for community service, practice, or applied work, and those of you looking to maximize both the theoretical and applied elements of your discipline might consider finding a home in a land-grant university that encourages and even requires involvement in the community and applied research. This can be an ideal blend for those who want a foot in both worlds. There is also the option of working in a job off the tenure track but doing some teaching or research on the side. One national study of contingent faculty concludes: "We were surprised by the extent we found they [the part-time faculty members] didn't want to be tenured or on the tenure track. As one participant who emphasized the advantages of eschewing the tenure track, 'I've been approached informally by members of our faculty to go tenure track, and I just said, "Forget it." I don't need that stress.' "[3]

Increasingly, colleges and universities have recruited PhDs outside of academia as faculty adjuncts, much as is done in medicine, law, and other professions that need to expose students to real-world experience. Thus, for PhDs who would like to avoid tenure-track pressures or who aren't able to land a job, there are many ways of maintaining intimate contact with the research and teaching in a university or college setting. If you elect this route, you probably should know that you may not always be accorded the full measure of respect that academics reserve for those inside the system, but many people simply do not care or even prefer to be part-time faculty, with less pressure to publish or teach a large number of courses.

Beyond the question of your particular passions, there are other good reasons why you might want to avoid academia. Academic life, especially at the top, pays very well these days, but it is not a particularly secure route to achieving monetary success. If you are the type of person who wants a job that you don't take home with you at night, this is yet another argument against academic life. Don't be tempted by the vision of evenings free and summers off; few academics that I've ever known manage to confine their working hours to nine to five. If you want job security, believe it or not, there are undoubtedly easier ways of finding it than by seeking tenure; you will be far better off finding a civil service position or even working in the private sector.

As I said in the preceding chapter, becoming a successful, and especially a contented, academic requires a certain temperament, skill set, passion, and determination that most people, even many of those who earn a PhD, do not possess. So when you complete your doctorate, you immediately face the critical decision of what kind of job to seek. Sometimes people let the marketplace make the choice. That is, they apply for both kinds of positions, letting their qualifications and potential employers decide for them. That is certainly an option, but I do not recommend it. You should think long and hard while you're completing your graduate work about what you want to do next and take the necessary steps to try to get the type of job that you want.

If you want an academic job and you strike out in the first round, as a certain number of recently minted PhD students invariably do, I wouldn't give up. By the same token, I would not necessarily take an academic job merely because you receive an offer. Remember what I said in the preceding chapter—you will probably only find academic life rewarding if you feel a very strong sense of commitment to the collegiate and scholarly ideals. Entering a teaching and research career is not a good choice, for example, if you have not enjoyed writing and publishing, unless you are fortunate enough to find a position that requires little or no active scholarship.

Many students, such as Rachel, wonder whether it is possible to enter the academic world after taking a non-academic job. It's neither easy nor common to attempt to enter a faculty position in mid-career, but it does happen more in some disciplines than others. Schools of public policy, management, education, health, and journalism, for example, are much more receptive to admitting seasoned veterans into their ranks than are many traditional academic disciplines, which erect higher barriers to those who lack a long record of scholarly publications.

The higher-educational newsletters provide ample testimony of the frustrations that people encounter when they attempt to shift course in mid-career and find a good academic position. The famous political historian and diplomat George F. Kennan discovered a wall of resistance from fellows at the Institute for Advanced Study at Princeton when his friend Robert J. Oppenheimer tried to recruit him. Despite a distinguished career in government, colleagues asked—rightly or not—what he had written of scholarly significance. Kennan only got the position because Oppenheimer used personal funds that were at his disposal as director of the Institute.[4]

The distinctions between the academic and non-academic worlds are not always as evident as some might think. Some non-academic jobs in science and social science, and even occasionally in the humanities, encourage or provide the opportunity to publish. Think, for example, of museum curators, scientists working for private industry, or economists employed by the federal government as good examples of non-academics whose jobs often require publishing in academic journals. Not surprisingly, jobs that bridge the boundaries between scholarly research and real-world settings are often the ones that give the greatest leeway for returning to a full-time academic career later in life. The coin of the realm that provides passage back into academia is publication and scholarly recognition. Attractive as they may be, few quasi-academic jobs provide the time and resources to amass a strong scholarly record, so it is important to avoid this route if you really aspire to a full-time teaching position later in your career, unless you are able to land one of the positions bridging the two worlds. Otherwise, you are better off looking for an adjunct position where you can fulfill your teaching and scholarly desires. Occasionally, holding an adjunct position of this sort can in fact lead to a tenure-track position, but don't count on it.

Most students know which direction they're headed by the time they are close to completing their degree. Graduate school provides, if not requires, exposure to jobs outside the confines of the university.[5] Although I could not locate reliable and detailed data on work patterns during graduate training, I daresay that regardless of discipline, many, if not most, students have held non-academic jobs related to their graduate degree before or during their time in graduate school. In the humanities, it may be editing, language instruction or translation, or research in a non-academic setting; in social science, consulting, work with nonprofits, and jobs with research organizations are common ways of supplementing income during summers or as alternatives to teaching or research fellowships; in the sciences, government and industry often provide part-time employment for individuals on a PhD track. Students who are contemplating a non-academic placement after getting their degrees should explore job possibilities while in graduate school. Frequently faculty can offer contacts, and sharp-eyed professionals outside of academic settings are often on the lookout for future recruits. Graduates students, whether cognizant of it or not, are deciding the direction of their careers by how they spend their time while in graduate school.

Working outside of academia while in graduate school, or at least making contacts in the non-academic world when you are still a student, demonstrates the right kind of interest to potential employers outside of teaching departments. I say outside of teaching departments because many non-academic careers are, in fact, located in colleges and universities in administration or research labs, or in programs in a university or university-like community in science centers or research units that may be formally or informally attached to universities. Indeed, many of these "non-academic" jobs may offer a lot of the benefits of academic life, such as good working conditions and congenial environments, without the grinding pressures of a tenure-track position. These positions constitute a more appealing part of the world of adjunct positions and represent a viable way for many PhDs to enjoy the fruits of the academic world without requiring the kind of commitment to publishing required in most tenure-track positions and even many non-tenure-track jobs. Unlike the itinerant adjuncts who are looking for a more permanent and stable position, these adjunct positions often come with good job security and reasonable benefits attached to a non-academic position.

Although I have mentioned that non-academic jobs often afford opportunities for research, mentoring, and even teaching, non-academic PhDs can also be openly suspicious if not disdainful of putting too high a premium on academic culture. Some non-academic employers, sometimes led by individuals who had either fled the academic world or failed to succeed in it, may be looking for a different sort of attitude and temperament in their younger colleagues. The advice columns in the trade journals of higher education are replete with stories about what happened when an unsuspecting candidate for a position in a non-academic setting came unprepared for an interview.

Christine Kelley, a graduate student career consultant, mentions a few typical questions that betray the cultural divide between academic and non-academic jobs. "Why aren't you applying to academic jobs?" "Most of your co-workers won't have PhDs, so how are you going to effectively communicate with them?" "How are you going to be able to work in a team environment?" and "How did getting your PhD prepare you for this job?"[6] Note the assumptions behind the questions: academically oriented individuals may be too asocial, self-regarding, and ill prepared to function in a non-academic setting. Whether this is true or not, if you are headed for a non-academic job with a PhD, you had better be ready to deal with the occasional display of social stereotyping. A sense of humor may serve you well in job interviews and later on in your work setting.

FACING THE ACADEMIC ALTERNATIVES: WHAT COUNTS?

In the current climate of austerity, you will often hear (evidenced by the title of a recent article) that "Every Ph.D. Needs a Plan B."[7] But a Plan B need not invariably be a non-academic position if your heart is set on working as a teacher and researcher. Academic positions exist in many strata, ranging from elite universities to community colleges. Looming in the future is the possibility that higher education will be turned over to the for-profit sector, which typically employs low-cost approaches to learning. Even before the Great Recession of 2007–2008, tenured positions and even full-time employment, especially tenure-track positions, in four-year universities and colleges had been disappearing at a rapid clip even while the total number of faculty positions has increased. In 1970 more than two-thirds of all academic jobs were on the tenure track. By 2007 this proportion had been cut by more than half. It is important to note that this does not imply that the absolute number of tenure-track jobs has been declining, though that could happen in the future. In fact, the *absolute number* of full-time tenure-track jobs continues to grow: it increased significantly over the ten-year period of 1997–2007 from 395,000 to 429,000 (although the number of applicants during this same period grew even more rapidly). Overall, there were far more instructional positions, even full-time jobs, created over that ten-year period, but a smaller percentage of them came with the benefits of tenure.[8] Without the obvious attractions of tenure, most full-time, non-tenure-track teaching positions still can provide good benefits such as a manageable teaching load, time and rewards for research, and good colleagueship. However, many PhDs regard these less exclusive jobs as distinctly second-choice alternatives if they seek a career in higher education, because jobs off the tenure track may not afford the same level of autonomy and self-direction provided to those on a tenure track and often have more demanding teaching and service loads at the same time that they offer lower salaries and fewer benefits.[9] A growing number of faculty positions are part-time and designed to attract people holding non-academic jobs who want to teach part-time. Even worse, a growing number of these adjunct positions provide little pay and few rewards. This may be fine as long as you have a good day job, but otherwise they are generally a poor substitute for a tenure-track position or a full-time academic job that is not on the tenure track.

In the current climate of budget austerity and cutbacks, it is easy to see why these non-traditional positions in higher education are growing faster than tenure-track jobs, but the degradation of academic jobs may not continue indefinitely. There are some grounds for optimism for a period of growth in faculty positions in the intermediate future. Until the last couple of decades, the United States has provided a model for higher education that the rest of the world has emulated. We have an attractive mix of public and private schools, universities and four-year colleges, and a huge network of two-year community colleges that offer a low-cost pathway to a four-year degree or an associate degree, which often provides necessary technical training for a good-paying job.

Tight as times are now, it is difficult not to foresee a healthy amount of expansion in these institutions during the next decades. The massive impending retirement of the baby boomer academics who filled an expanding higher-education system in the 1970s and 1980s will create a number of openings in the next two decades. Moreover, the universities without strong research programs, which are often funded by state and local government, will have to grow if the United States is going to remain competitive in a global economy that is expanding the need for higher education worldwide. There will undoubtedly be more global cooperation in educating students from abroad. Many readers of this book may come to divide their time between academic life in this country and abroad, a not-so-unattractive prospect for a younger or senior PhD who is committed to a teaching and research career.

Of course, a good deal of future employment may depend on the viability of distance learning and online courses, a trend that is currently sweeping academia. Debates rage over whether distance learning or online courses as a supplement to classroom teaching may be used to bring down the costs of higher education. At this early stage, we simply do not know how this very recent development in higher education will play out and whether it will lead to sizable downsizing of faculty in universities and colleges.

So yes, have a Plan B that allows for the possibility of not getting a choice job immediately, but if you are committed to teaching and research, you need not get out of the academic business entirely. However, the options before you require very different strategies. Particularly, if your heart is set on teaching at a ranking university or college, then you must pursue your goal differently than if you prefer, or are at least willing to settle for, a less prestigious academic position.

Why would anyone *prefer* a position that typically offers less accomplished students, less money, less time off, and fewer resources— features that often characterize jobs in teaching institutions that do not emphasize research or positions in the community college system?[10] In fact, most PhDs reach as far as they can to find a "good" position, but definitions of a "good" position certainly vary, as I can attest from watching the many students that I've advised and mentored over the years. First of all, many PhDs starting out in their professional careers want a job that comes with a life outside of work. They may well prefer a less competitive university, for example, that provides both a good work environment and a quality setting to a top-ranked institution that is located in an undesirable place or promises the pressures of a tenure-track job that may be ultimately unattainable.

Years ago a very talented student of mine, I'll call him John Kassen, was on the job market in a good year when he might well have landed a position in one of the best departments. He had several publications in good journals and superior recommendations from his mentors. However, John accepted the first job he was offered, early in the hiring season, which was a position in a good but not leading department. When I asked him why he didn't hold out to see what else would come his way, he replied with some anger and resentment to my question: "It is a good job. I think that I can get tenure without getting stressed out. Besides it's a great location and a wonderful place to raise a family." As soon as he stormed out of my office, I realized that he was absolutely right. My question implied that a more prestigious place would necessarily be a better job fit for him. I conceded to him later in the day that my question contained an arrogant, and I believe inaccurate, assumption that institutional ranking trumps other considerations. Now, years later, when both of us look back on that encounter, we can laugh about it. John has found a wonderful home in a good department and leads just the kind of balanced life he always wanted.

A lot of different considerations figure in the mix of making a good decision in your first job choice if you are pursuing an academic career. Work and family balance is high on the list. Most full-time academics work hard, but some are psychologically prepared to work very long hours and others simply cannot accept having work crowd out many other parts of life, especially family time.[11]

By the end of graduate school, most students know pretty well how high they want to aspire and how hard they are willing to work to achieve their goals. A lot of recent PhDs are really looking for a good teaching post and do not want to devote much time or energy, if any at all, to doing scholarly research and writing after completing their doctorate. Perhaps as many as a majority of PhDs will never publish anything after their thesis is completed![12] Although this category of unpublished PhDs includes those who are frustrated and discontented with their lack of scholarly productivity because they cannot find the time to pursue research and writing in their work life, many others have decided happily or perhaps wistfully that scholarship, at least the production side of it, is not for them. They are content to be consumers, purveyors, and perhaps critics in their respective disciplines. Their passion is for exposing students to important ideas and scholarly materials, making judicious use of what appears in the journals of their profession, and introducing the tenets of their field to undergraduates. Doing that well can be and often is a source of deep satisfaction, and it plays an important part in the workings of the higher-education system by training and recruiting future academics and, more broadly, creating an audience for their scholarship.

The prospect of teaching in a state system but not at the flagship locale, a small but not well-endowed college campus, a community college that primarily attracts first-generation college students, perhaps even a private secondary school that caters to talented high school students can offer huge gratifications to able teachers with a PhD. And many places are congenial settings for such a mission. The variation within the institutional stratum of colleges and universities that do not require their faculty to produce a steady flow of research publications is enormous. There are well-run community colleges and local four-year colleges and universities just as there are poorly run elite graduate programs.[13] Departmental life can be pleasant and rewarding or toxic and mind-numbing at all levels in higher education. Many people are surprised to learn that job satisfaction in surveys of academics is at most only weakly related to the type or ranking of the institutional setting. This suggests that academics gravitate to institutions that serve their needs and aspirations, or, perhaps, that most of us are capable of being satisfied with what life offers us.[14]

I don't want to cast too rosy a light on the job situations because there is a sizable academic underclass of PhDs who make a living by teaching courses part-time at multiple institutions to which they are only weakly attached because there is no attempt to integrate them into the life of the department or even to provide office space where they can meet with their students. There is no denying that most of this segment of the adjunct population lives on subsistence wages and often lack the most meager of the usual amenities associated with a teaching job.

Only recently has there been sufficient attention given to the growing number of itinerant PhDs who are often being ruthlessly taken advantage of by higher-education employers who rely primarily or exclusively on part-time faculty. This book gives insufficient attention to this growing population who deserve better conditions than they receive and are often exploited by the institutions that employ them as a way of reducing costs. This academic underclass is gaining more attention, but they constitute an ugly underbelly of academic life. There is an appalling absence of information on the PhDs who are outside of academic institutions. Some itinerant faculty may work their way into permanent positions, but many remain adrift without adequate ties to the institutions that they serve. We simply do not know, for example, just how many academics employed as adjuncts manage to find their way into a full-time position, much less a tenure-track job.

Understanding the alternatives once you have a PhD is, of course, a lot easier than locating a situation that offers reasonable benefits and a good fit for your interests. So you must be prepared to consider a number of questions such as the following: Where do you feel you want to be professionally and personally a decade from now? Where are you willing to live? What kinds of students will you find rewarding to teach and mentor? How central is your scholarly work to the rest of your life? If you are not shooting for the moon, then the search takes a very different form if you are heading for a research and teaching career at an institution that is primarily devoted to teaching undergraduates, especially a community college or non-select, local four-year college.

You must have no illusions about one thing: your first job will have important consequences for your next one, assuming, as I do, that most of you will not remain at the same place your entire career. In fact, few of us do. I am one of a relatively small percentage of academics I know who has spent their entire career in the same place, although I often observe that it feels like I have been in four or five different departments during my tenure in the sociology department at Penn because I've seen so many colleagues come and go over the years and been through so much change in the culture of departmental life.

It must be perfectly obvious to most readers that it is far easier to move from a better-ranked institution to a lower-ranked one than vice versa. Even if you are disinclined to reach up, there are good reasons for doing so when you consider your first position if you want to have more latitude to move later on. For example, it is very difficult, although not impossible, to move from a community college to a four-year institution or from a bottom-tier institution to a much better ranked university. Contacts and networks always help, but in all likelihood, the escape route involves publishing. And the support for publishing is often in short supply at lower-rung institutions.

WHEN TO START A FAMILY (IF EVER)?

Most people finish their PhD in their late twenties (the pattern of scientists and social scientists) or early thirties (more in the humanities) if they enter graduate school within a year or two of completing college. However, some readers will have entered graduate school after they have established a lasting partnership and perhaps had children. But for those who have not, the biological clock is ticking for women who want children, and it is certainly relevant for men as well who may not want to wait to start a family until they are in midlife. Is there an ideal time for an academic to have a family? I would answer that there are probably worse times to have children, such as the very beginning of entering graduate school or when first entering a teaching position, and generally better times, such as during a postdoc or after getting settled in a suitable job. Yet there is no single pattern that will suit all. Some people more cynical than I might answer that question by saying that there is really no good time, but I don't agree. I've watched my students and young people that I've mentored over the years and have concluded that the right time depends as much on personal considerations as it does on institutional considerations.

Like many parts of academic life, gender often figures into such decisions.[15] The question of timing is almost invariably more salient for women than men, who have greater latitude to defer having children and frequently do not assume the major responsibilities of parenthood, not to mention the rigors of childbearing and infant care. Therefore, I will focus on the circumstances of women academics in this section.

When I entered academia, women were few in number and most were in adjunct positions in colleges and universities, especially if they were parents. Happily, this is no longer true in my field of sociology and indeed in the majority of academic specialties outside of some of the physical sciences, engineering, and an assortment of other disciplines. Women are now the majority of recent PhDs, and their percentage has grown at all ranks—though not nearly quickly enough in the opinion of many.[16] Moreover, a growing number of younger women have children while attending graduate school, in the postdoctoral period, or as assistant professors. Only a minor fraction can defer parenthood until after tenure, if only because they are by then usually in their late thirties or early forties. Still, although the circumstances for academic parents have greatly improved over my lifetime, most mothers, and a growing number of fathers, still struggle with finding the right balance between work and family.

In this respect, they are no different than other professional and nonprofessional parents in American society, where balancing work and family demands is left pretty much up to individuals to make the best situation that they can. In fact, colleges and universities generally provide more congenial environments to have and raise children than do most other professional occupations. Institutions of higher education typically have more generous workplace policies than other occupational settings, enabling mothers to take maternity leave sometimes with pay, or at least, as federal law now requires, without sacrificing their positions. Still, it is rough going for female academics because they cannot easily put their careers on hold while they start a family.[17]

Having a child before or during graduate school works for some people if they are in a stable relationship where they can share responsibilities. Needless to say, it is a lot harder for single parents unless they have support from their families while they are in school and caring for children. It is undeniably difficult to take classes, study for exams, and write a dissertation while parenting a young child, but I've seen a lot of women manage these parental responsibilities and perform excellently at the same time. Obviously, it helps to be partnered with the right person and to be in a supportive institutional context. Increasingly, there is more social support by faculty for graduate students who are parents, but it remains true that in some fields and some departments, subtle or not-so-subtle forms of bias persist, including difficulty procuring TA positions or fellowships.[18] But it is far easier to fight these forms of discrimination than it was in the not-so-distant past.

A growing number of couples begin their academic careers in commuter marriages, no easy feat particularly especially if they already have children.[19] If they are both academics, as is frequently the case, it may be difficult to find two positions in the same locale or within a reasonable distance.[20] While these commuter unions are trying, couples sometimes manage to use them to their advantage by working long hours when they are apart in order to spend more time together when they are not. Not being in the same place as their partner is another reason why many women prefer to delay childbearing until they are reasonably settled rather than make immediate compromises in their job options. It is a tough choice for which there is no standard prescription.

I've known a number of women who enter parenthood during a postdoctoral post, particularly if their position could be extended by a maternity leave. It is a relatively lower-stress period in academic life and may provide a bit more latitude in your schedule than having a child at the same time that you begin a full-time teaching job. My advice is to talk it over with your academic supervisor unless it is a *fait accompli* or you have reason to believe he or she will be unsympathetic to your having a child during your postdoctoral years. Of course, there can be delicate legal issues in trying to influence a student's parental decisions, so tread carefully: you may be left to infer how your mentors will feel about your decision. It is obviously wise to consult university parental leave policies as you think through the best way of timing your transition to parenthood.

Some women scale down their ambitions after they have a child to accommodate the realities of parenthood. This strategy also has its pitfalls. It is frequently difficult to return to full-time academic life unless you are able to publish while teaching part-time or you have an understanding with your academic institution. However, it is also the case that many PhDs, female and male alike, prefer a smaller workload while they are raising children to maintain their sanity. Surveys of academics show that varying levels of satisfaction were reported, not surprisingly, in faculty working part-time and in non-tenure-track positions.[21] Some women feel that they have the best of both worlds, teaching or doing research part-time while they raise a family. For now, it is sufficient to say that there is no one way of managing parenthood in academia that is best suited for all.

FINDING THE "RIGHT" JOB

More ink is spilled in the trade journals of higher-education writing about the job search for recent PhDs than any other topic, except perhaps the tenure process. The transition from graduate school is rightly seen as a critical juncture that influences the shape of a young academic's subsequent career. Managing this transition successfully begins with the selection of a graduate program and continues during your training in graduate school. The choice of a specialty in your discipline, of advisors, and of a dissertation topic will all influence your prospects later on.

Most of all, your existing record, particularly your record of publications as a graduate student, will likely affect your placement in the job market; or if you are going for a position in a teaching university, it is critical to have a strong record of experience in the classroom. The rest is largely cosmetic: how you present yourself in your letters of application and in the interview.

To be sure, this presentation is not trivial. You have to get in the door, and advice columns and guidebooks contain endless discussions of how to increase your prospects of doing so. Yes, it is worth investing the time to write a convincing and coherent statement of your research interests, accomplishments, and teaching qualifications, but my point is that a lot of what you can say rests on what you have already done, not merely on what you hope to do in the future. Yes, it matters who writes letters of recommendation for you and what they have to say, but again you largely select your sponsors by your choice of advisors in graduate school and the research mentors that you have already acquired. Most of all, I repeat that having a record of publication by the time you leave graduate school will increase the odds of getting a job, especially in a Tier I or II research university or an attractive undergraduate institution.

The job market varies tremendously from discipline to discipline. In many sciences and social sciences, there is still a relatively good balance between openings and job aspirants. In the humanities, this is often not true, and programs continue to churn out more candidates than there are positions. This means that the number of unemployed or underemployed part-time candidates can reach alarming proportions in poor economic times, as occurred in the period after the Great Recession of 2007–2008. In the sciences and to a growing extent in the social sciences, there are attractive opportunities for PhDs outside of the mainstream market of four-year colleges and universities. This helps keep some balance in the job market because colleges and universities must compete with private industry and nonprofits that need talented researchers. The most recent National Science Foundation report on doctorate degrees reveals that roughly two-thirds of doctorates have definite job prospects at the time they receive the degrees. This level is somewhat lower than before the recent recession. If the economy continues to heal, the prospects of recent PhDs will improve and may reach the pre-recession level, where closer to three-fourths of doctorates will have a definite position by the time they receive their degree. There is, of course, variation in these figures by field, but generally speaking only those in the humanities fare significantly worse. Even so, more than half of doctoral recipients in the humanities have a firm job commitment by the time they are awarded their PhD.[22]

Education trade journals have given increasing attention to considering the huge number of positions in two-year and local four-year institutions that are training a hefty and growing number of undergraduates. Admittedly, some readers may consider teaching at a community college or a local four-year institution a step down, but, as I noted earlier, many such places provide reasonable job conditions and eager students. One thing to keep in mind is that these open-door institutions are looking almost exclusively for engaging and passionately committed teachers who can handle a heavy teaching load. If that is not in your skill set, you should consider a non-academic job or perhaps an administrative position in a college or university.

There was once a time when students didn't need to publish while in graduate school even if they expected to do so later on in their careers. That time has probably ended if you are seeking a tenure-track position: if you have not published during graduate school, it is commonly assumed that you are unlikely to do so after you complete your dissertation. This is certainly truer in some fields than in others. In many disciplines, especially the humanities, the dissertation is frequently the first publication and often will provide the necessary down payment for demonstrating your potential for future scholarly productivity. But in most sciences and social sciences, it is now expected that you will publish at least an article or two, and sometimes many more, on the way to getting your degree if you want a job at a top-tier or second-tier university or a selective college.

Some years ago when my department advertised for an assistant professor, someone had the bright idea of inviting a couple of graduate students to witness the process as part of their professional socialization. It was a disaster! I watched with dismay the ashen faces of the graduate students as the faculty whipped through a large pile of applications sorting out the expectant and young PhDs, discarding résumés that had no publications almost automatically unless they came from top-ranked schools and contained outstanding letters. Even so, few if any candidates survived without a record of publication. I had to explain to the shocked students, who were in the early years of their training, that their résumés would grow in time, but it was a hard lesson for these newcomers to academia.

Mind you, it was not always this way. Decades ago, when I got my job at Penn, many people were hired even before they had finished their thesis, and it was relatively unusual then, at least in my field, to publish before completing a degree. This is no longer true, and it has raised the stakes for getting a position at a top-tier research university or a ranking liberal arts college, even if the candidate comes out of a highly touted graduate program. In some fields, the expectations for publication have become ridiculously high, creating a false sense of scholarly accomplishment where more is not always better as a professional work style. Still, there is no denying that these lofty standards are leading departments to demand a substantial demonstration that a candidate is capable of being tenured before they are hired. This drives many students from ranking departments, if they are relatively unpublished, to consider a postdoctoral position as an intermediate step. It provides a way for talented fledgling academics to build up their résumés while they gain more research experience, giving them time to write without contending with a full schedule of teaching and departmental responsibilities. There is much to be said—even for students who have enough of a publishing record to get a good job—for doing a postdoc, if only because it provides a more gradual transition into the demands of being an assistant professor.

SEEKING A POSTDOCTORAL FELLOWSHIP

A postdoc is a well-designed professional stage between graduate school and a first teaching post because it provides the leisure to test and refine research and writing skills in a relatively low-pressure environment. In many of the sciences, postdocs are virtually required and are increasingly recommended in the social sciences for students who are being groomed for jobs in the best and better departments. Regrettably, postdocs are still more scarce in the social sciences and rarer still in the humanities. About 70 percent of doctorates in the life sciences move to a postdoc, compared to 60 percent of those in the physical sciences, 40 percent in the social sciences and engineering, and only a tenth of those in other fields, including the humanities.[23]

Departments often resist hiring a newly minted PhD in large part because recruiting from the pool of postdocs and assistant professors offers significant advantages. From the perspective of the hiring departments, it frequently makes sense to recruit someone with greater professional maturity, a stronger record of publications, and a wider network of mentors and sponsors who are able to provide testimony of his or her scholarly potential. And for young PhDs, a postdoc provides an advanced apprenticeship that can offer mentoring and supervision before you are fully autonomous, not to mention a chance to beef up your vita.

The opportunities for postdoctoral work have grown in the past several decades, extending beyond the sciences to the social sciences and occasionally in the humanities. A recent count of postdocs in the sciences, engineering, health professions, and the social sciences counted more than 67,000 students in postdoctoral positions in 2010, an increase of 45 percent over the previous decade, suggesting that the number of postdoctoral positions in these fields are increasing at a rate similar to the growth in PhDs.[24] Supported by government and foundation funding, many leading departments have training grants or research projects directed by faculty. Independent research institutions, policy centers, and individual researchers also provide postdocs to promising students who can contribute to their ongoing research agenda. These institutions tend to recruit from the leading graduate programs, but they sometimes provide positions to talented students from less prestigious programs, a route to upward mobility for PhDs who can then launch their careers from a loftier place.

Despite the obvious advantages of having an interlude between graduate school and an academic position, some postdocs are not as attractive as others: some programs provide much better training, support, and resources than others. At best, a postdoctoral position can provide an excellent opportunity to augment a recent PhD's professional training by exposing him or her to new ideas, a chance to learn new techniques and skills, and most of all a chance to put publications in the pipeline. The leading postdoctoral fellowships are regarded as an indication of high academic promise and a gateway to the best departments in a given discipline. At worst, a postdoctoral program can exploit and alienate younger scholars either because they are left to their own devices without adequate supervision or training or because young PhDs are inappropriately yoked to projects that are largely designed to advance the interests of established researchers who will derive most of the credit for the work. Look carefully for programs that have a good record of placement, where former students speak well of the support they were given, there are opportunities for independent research, and postdocs generally leave with publications.

Obviously, a two-year program is far better than a single year unless the latter is at the same place as you did your graduate work. In the sciences, four-year and five-year postdocs are common, but in the social sciences they generally do not last more than two years. Relocating, getting to know a new place, and continuing your research agenda, much less beginning new projects, all take time, and it is far more challenging to accomplish much in a one-year program than a longer-duration program. This requires some planning while you are still in graduate school: by the time you are writing your dissertation, you should have a clear idea of postdoctoral possibilities.

There are some things that you can do to make the most of your postdoc, even if it is a brief one. It helps a lot to plan your year with a well-worked-out schedule, and you can do some of this planning even before you arrive. Figure out realistically what you can get done in the time that you have and try to adhere to your timetable. This means setting a list of priorities that you expect to complete and sticking to it. Keep in mind that you will have a lot of attractive distractions along the way: unforeseen opportunities to work with someone, new ideas for research, possibilities for travel and investigation. The trick is to balance these against the need to get articles from your thesis, complete unfinished papers, or write a grant proposal that will fund a future research project. Your mentors may not be completely disinterested in helping you make these choices if they develop a personal stake in your list of priorities—for example, wanting you to work on their research projects exclusively. Therefore it is wise to consult widely when you are working out your agenda beyond the postdoc.

How much can you expect to accomplish during a postdoctoral year or two? The answer to this question will vary greatly depending on your field and your placement, but one way to gauge it is to look at the record of work completed by former and senior postdocs in that program. Remember, though, that a postdoc will not enhance your job prospects unless you leave it with publications and strong endorsements from your mentors. Typically, quality of publication trumps quantity—that is, placement in top journals and influence through recognition and citations. At the beginning of an academic career, these judgments are a bit more forgiving: evaluators want to see evidence of scholarly promise, such as imagination in finding a good problem, intelligent use of novel or cutting-edge analytic techniques, and the ability to build a research agenda that extends into the future. Publication matters, but early in your career the writing—and especially its acceptance for publication in reasonable places—and recognition through grants are all widely accepted as indications of scholarly promise. There are many ways of using your postdoctoral years intelligently, and even more ways of using these years unwisely.

Postdoctoral students frequently asked me about the value of collaborative work, especially when they are not the first author, versus work that they publish on their own. There is no definitive answer, because it will depend on the nature of the collaboration, the publication outlet, and the intellectual quality of the work. But it is critical that you be the first or sole author on some of your work during your postdoc. A good mentor will find a way to make this happen. In any event, if you haven't already done so, a postdoc provides time to publish from your thesis.

Postdoctoral time, like a sabbatical, seems to go more quickly than ordinary time. As I said, it is critical to have tangible products to show for your experience by the end of your postdoc. This is another juncture where you can assess, looking at your own experience, whether it makes sense to consider a non-academic job or to readjust your expectations of the level of institution where you think you are likely to find a job. If you have not produced much during your postdoctoral career, you must ask yourself whether it is realistic to seek or expect a job at a top-tier institution, or even a second-tier research university, because potential employers will surely be making the same sort of assessment. It is important to bring your expectations in line with what you are realistically capable of accomplishing. Otherwise, you may be destined for disappointment in your academic career.

THE SEARCH FOR AN ACADEMIC POSITION

When I was hired at Penn some decades ago, the rules of recruitment were vastly different from today. Information about jobs was not posted or widely circulated. Mostly, new faculty members were recruited through letters announcing an opening to colleagues and professional friends, what is now known as the "old boys' network." I visited one institution and had an hour-long chat with the chair of the department and several of his colleagues, who possibly constituted a search committee but might have been just a few trusted advisors. At the end of the hour, he offered me a position that I decided not to take. My job at Penn came about through a letter from one member of the department to my dissertation chair. On the basis of my mentor's recommendation, I visited Penn and had lunch with some of the faculty, where I was invited to discuss my research plans for a few minutes. Later in the day I met with some faculty, who chatted with me informally. That was it.

As far as I know, no one systematically reviewed my dossier, although one or two people had seen an article that I recently had published in a leading journal in sociology. I got an offer the following week.

Now the system for hiring has become highly structured by rules and procedure. Jobs must be announced publicly in disciplinary newsletters and other outlets. Faculty members are often encouraged to contact colleagues, as they did in the old days, but the department or the academic institution often regulates these contacts. The search process is carefully monitored to ensure that there is no discrimination and that a designated committee of faculty has access to applicant files. As far as I can tell, this is all to the good because it widens the pool of applicants and puts everyone on an equal footing, at least in theory. This doesn't prevent a certain amount of informal communication or lobbying by mentors for their promising students. This happens all the time at professional meetings and through e-mail and the like. So the professional network continues to operate as a backdrop to the hiring process, and personal testimony on behalf of students by their sponsors continues to have an influence, but there is far more scrutiny of the hiring process than there was several decades ago to ensure its fairness.

The process begins with the announcement of an opening in a variety of professional outlets, which typically describes the level of the appointment and often states a priority in a special sub-area of the discipline. Applicants sometimes ignore the emphasis on a special field, and it does sometimes happen that departments, too, disregard their announced preferences. But this doesn't happen very often, and I counsel my students not to apply for positions for which they are manifestly unqualified. Sometimes a job posting contains a very specific description that suggests that the department knows exactly who they want to hire and are merely going through the motions of opening up the search. There's no harm in applying for jobs that are "wired," but don't hold out too much hope of getting them. This more often happens for senior- than for junior-level appointments. If you have contacts with the department through your mentors and sponsors, it is often possible to find out just how open the search is and how much the wording of the announcement will determine the outcome of the search.

Sometimes announcements are supplemented by letters from a department chair or search committee asking for nominations and recommendations for a particular post. This provides an opportunity for your mentors to put in a good word for you to the search committee in advance of the formal review process and to indicate your qualifications. But unlike in the past, the formal application process begins with a published job listing to which candidates are invited to apply, usually with a letter of inquiry and often a curriculum vita, sometimes accompanied by a statement of experience and approach to teaching or writing samples. Be sure to ask at least one of your mentors to review your materials before you send them out. Search committees may also ask for letters of recommendation at this early stage of review, but they sometimes wait until the initial round of screening has been completed. Even if letters are not required, informal communications from the members of your dissertation committee or other mentors can help you get in the door, or at least through the initial review.

Search committees, and occasionally full departments especially if they are small, will almost always sort through a long list of applicants that sometimes are in the hundreds to identify a smaller pool, a first cut of the applicants, whom they scrutinize with greater care. Making the "short list," as it is often referred to, signals that they are taking your application for the job seriously. It is a big step and can be regarded as a signal to you that you are in contention for the position. At the same time, it is important to realize that getting on the short list, which sometimes contains as many as ten or fifteen applicants, is still often only a preliminary step to getting an interview. You may not even hear about this first stage, as the list is typically further whittled down after letters of recommendation are received and search committees read writing samples.

These days most initial interviews, especially at institutions with limited budgets, may occur by telephone. It can be a harrowing experience to be interviewed at long distance by unseen faculty, who shoot questions into the phone that you must answer virtually without pause. Similarly, in some departments a certain amount of screening occurs at professional meetings, where candidates may have a fifteen- or thirty-minute interview with several members of the department in a face-to-face encounter. Some students describe the experience of these preliminary interviews as being akin to speed dating.

These early interviews can be hit or miss and can feel uncomfortably superficial if not downright dismissive. The only strategy is to practice your responses to questions that have a predictable form: "Why did you choose to work on this topic for your dissertation?" "Describe the intellectual contributions that came out of your thesis." "What is your research agenda for the next few years?" "How would you organize the introductory course?" And so on. Sometimes you have already answered these exact questions in the materials that you submitted, but be ready to repeat your answers in a poised manner.

Departments and training centers are much better than they used to be in preparing students for these initial encounters. Often they provide workshops helping students to go on the market, a practice that only started in the last couple of decades, at least in my field. If you do not have access to this type of preparation, it is easy enough for you and your fellow students to put a practice session together. You may be able to get sympathetic faculty to join in.

Announcements of openings usually occur sometime in the late summer or early fall, and there is typically a period of a couple of months before the initial recruitment period is closed. It is a bad idea to procrastinate in organizing your application, so your dossier should be complete no later than summer's end. It often happens that departments lower down in the rankings try to recruit earlier to pick off some of the attractive candidates by offering jobs before the bigger fish move in. The recruitment season typically occurs in the fall and early winter, but some positions are not authorized and announced until later in the year, providing a second season for job searches that lingers into the spring.

The winnowing down of the short list can be a mysterious and sometimes arbitrary process because search committees frequently do it by adding up the subjective evaluations of a handful of people whose preferences do not always reflect the same criteria. Yet I've always been surprised to see the degree of concordance rather than its absence in committees that I've served on over the years. Getting from ten contenders to three or four candidates who will be invited to visit the department involves a lot of reading and discussion, and sometimes includes internal bargaining and trade-offs within the committee or between subcommittees seeking different positions within a department.

Crunch time for both departments and candidates occurs when the interviews begin, as departments must select among the candidates interviewed and candidates often face multiple job offers. Many have suggested that recruitment would be a lot less hazardous for both parties if they adopted a system like the one used for selecting medical interns and residents, where departments and candidates are matched by ranking their choices. But academic searches have not yet adopted this more rational approach, though it is being widely considered in the field of economics. As it stands now, the process is typically protracted and unwieldy, creating a high degree of uncertainty and apprehension by job candidates.

In the past decade, job blogs have started in many fields that reduce some of the uncertainty as candidates provide information and feedback on the process to one another. Only rarely do departments provide early feedback on their selections to the entire field, informing applicants that they are no longer being considered for a position. Word of mouth through these job blogs or surmising from the passage of time is about the only way that candidates learn whether they are not being considered for a specific job. Otherwise, candidates may only hear months later after the position has been filled.

THE CAMPUS INTERVIEW

Hiring does not always involve a campus interview, but it is still the main way that recruitment occurs, especially at the junior faculty level and at most four-year institutions. There is inevitably a certain amount of academic ceremony in the process, as departments are generally out to impress the candidates and show off their attractions. At the same time, they are doing due diligence in the search and giving the candidates careful professional and personal scrutiny. Although these rituals often have a compelling quality, they can also be disasters in departments in which tensions and disunity prevail. I can remember many years ago when my own department was so fractured by intellectual and personal disagreements that a job candidate confessed to me at the end of the day that he could not understand how younger faculty survived in my department. His sympathy was cold comfort for those of us trying to put on a brave face.

Standard preparation for a job interview now includes a practice talk at the candidate's home department before going on the road. Do not try to wing it because the job talk is usually the most important event in an interview. Be sure that you do a practice talk even if it is to a small group of fellow students. Usually, mentors will join in, and it generally proves to be a good way of ironing out complications in organization, exposing weaknesses in the argument or presentation of evidence, and achieving a good balance in the amount of information that you will present in the job talk.

I suspect that few readers, unless they have gone through this process already, realize how central the job talk is to the hiring process. Most of the audience, including the faculty outside the search committee, will be largely unfamiliar with you and your work. So it is usually worthwhile to spend a minute or so introducing your work and topic to people unacquainted with them. Try to set your talk in a larger context of your intellectual agenda and borrow successful approaches that you have seen in colloquia and professional talks during your training. In some sciences, following the formal presentation, candidates are asked to give an informal "chalk talk" where they discuss their intellectual ambitions and immediate research plans. These informal sessions, I am told, play an important part in the hiring process.

The most common error in a job talk is trying to do too much, such as summarizing a problem that is not easily contained in a talk of forty-five minutes or so, but sometimes candidates err in the opposite direction and say too little. Another frequent failing is to spend too much time on the windup and not enough on the delivery. Rushing through evidence because of an overlong introduction is a deadly sin but not an uncommon one in academic talks. Too much informality strikes some of the audience as superficial while too much formality could come across as pompous. You are looking for the perfect combination of balance and equanimity. Nervousness at the outset is usually forgiven at such occasions, but you want to come across as authoritative in your subject but willing to concede to questioners who point out valid criticisms. How well you respond to comments and critiques is no less important than the talk itself.

Departmental talks are structured by the differences in disciplinary cultures, and you should be well acquainted with them by the time you go on the job market. In some disciplines, frequent interruptions and questioning occur during the talk; in others, interruptions, aside from questions of clarification, are anathema. But you must be prepared for the occasional obnoxious faculty member who violates the standards and raises the eyebrows of his or her colleagues. A now-departed faculty member in my department was notorious for asking candidates whether they were familiar with his work, which was often only tangentially related to the topic. Such is life, and candidates will get a flavor of how the department operates in public situations. Assuming that you have some choice of where to go, it is not a bad thing to observe.

The job talk is usually the centerpiece of your visit, but the recruitment ritual typically involves meeting extensively with faculty one on one and in an informal dinner, lunch, or breakfast. There is lots of advice out there for managing these recruitment events; mine is simply to be yourself and hope that the fit is a good one. Common sense and good manners should dictate your behavior. Of course, it is unwise to be overly familiar with potential colleagues whom you do not know or to look for information about your competitors. And, yes, it is worthwhile to read up on the work of faculty members you are likely to meet, if only so that you can have a good intellectual discussion, something that most academics relish. Have as much fun as you possibly can, even though the circumstances of meeting a long string of scrutinizing faculty may not be everyone's cup of tea. Figure that the recruitment ritual gives you a chance to imagine that you might actually become part of the scene you are viewing. It is a reasonable way of discovering whether the position is plausible or even desirable.

You'll usually have a chance on the tour to talk to graduate or undergraduate students, and sometimes departments request that you give a class on your work. Graduate students, like some faculty, often are looking for intellectual comrades. Try to strike a proper balance between candor and circumspection: express your views but go easy on the strong opinions, which can be off-putting. In more than a few departments, graduate students wield considerable influence in hiring, either formally by membership on the search committee or informally in the feedback they may give faculty. Arrogance or dismissive attitudes toward students can be devastating to a candidate's chances.

You must assume that social forms of communication, such as Facebook and personal blogs, might be examined by students and faculty alike. What students share with one another during graduate school and beyond in semi-public venues, without sufficient safeguards for confidentiality, can now be scrutinized by larger audiences. One of my students recently told me that he was concerned about how others might view a former peer who freely shared opinions about his colleagues on his Facebook page.

Having watched scores of my former students go through the recruitment process and having witnessed numerous candidate visits over the years, I confess that it is difficult to predict the outcome of recruitment in advance. Whether you visit first or last, whether you have inside knowledge of the department or not, whether you are the leading candidate at the start or a dark horse, I've always found it difficult to guess who will make it to the finish line. Although it is hard not to take it personally if you are not the chosen one, keep in mind that there are invariably others with good qualifications. Being runner-up, though it may be cold comfort, does not mean that you were unqualified for the job or didn't handle the process well. Recruitment has a certain amount of arbitrary features that you cannot completely control. The very things that you hold most dear in your own academic life may not be universally shared. You may be surprised to discover huge differences in accepted values or what is taken for granted in a department different from the one in which you have been trained.

In any given year, there is always a fortunate subset of "hot" job candidates who garner a disproportionate amount of attention and have the luxury of touring many departments in quest of the "best position." As I've said repeatedly, academia is highly stratified, and departments are intensely competitive when it comes to landing these top prospects. The candidates almost invariably come from the leading departments and begin the search process with a certain amount of notoriety because they have published widely. Don't be intimated if you participate in the online chat groups. Most well-qualified candidates from good departments, even if they are not highly sought after, nonetheless end up finding good jobs. True, the situation in certain fields has been bleak in recent years. But we can say the same about graduates in law, some fields of business, and in other professions like architecture. Undeniably, there are up and down cycles for hiring over which you have little or no control.

The world of recruitment looks very different from the perspective of hot candidates who may face an embarrassment of riches when it comes to job offers. I mentioned earlier that often ambitious but lower-ranking departments get out of the gate earlier in the recruitment process and make offers before more highly ranked institutions complete the screening process. This creates a dilemma for the candidate. Mary Painter, a young collaborator of mine, encountered that situation several years ago when she was interviewed and was offered a job at one of the campuses of a state system while being recruited in another locale at a better state university. She faced the classic squeeze after her job offer came through with a short deadline for acceptance. I advised Mary to inform the chair of the other department promptly and see if the process could be hastened. Her interview date was moved up, and she was told that she was the leading candidate but that the administration had to approve the department's choice.

I suggested some legitimate ways of stalling, such as negotiating for conditions and asking for a letter in writing, which she did. Unfortunately, the deadline came with the matter still pending at the attractive alternative institution. Mary decided that she had to accept "the bird in hand," only to learn shortly thereafter that she was, in fact, offered the more desirable position. Although some candidates might have reversed their decision, Mary decided that she could not honorably change course after accepting the first position. Could she have done otherwise? Yes, but turning down a position that you've previously accepted would be considered professionally (though not legally in this case) inappropriate. The ethics of turning down a position after accepting it, in fact, are a bit ambiguous.[25]

NEGOTIATING THE TERMS OF EMPLOYMENT

The job offer usually initiates a bargaining process that often feels uncomfortable to the eager candidate. It is one thing to have multiple offers at hand and quite another to have a single offer. Yet even in the latter case, it is perfectly acceptable to counter an offer unless it is manifestly generous and complete. The conditions of employment matter, and many institutions do not put their best and final offer immediately on the table. They expect some dickering to take place. How much flexibility is there, and how extensively should you bargain after the initial offer? Private institutions usually have a bit more latitude in give and take than public institutions, which are often bound by stricter and more uniform rules when it comes to salary and work conditions. Still, there is often some room for maneuvering even when the conditions are relatively fixed.

Salary is obviously the key consideration for many, and it is important to realize that some extras that you may request are less important than salary because your initial base can determine what you will be making years later, as raises are often fixed percentages of your base, for example, "Everybody this year will get a salary increase of 2.77 percent." Institutions often prefer to add benefits in the form of a research account that may extend over several years. Just remember that $2,000 more in annual salary may better than a $5,000 slush fund to be spent over the following three years.

Time off is worth a lot, so a reduction in course load in the first years or the promise of an early sabbatical are high up on the list of faculty enticements because they provide the most precious of all benefits: time to write. Early in a career, time makes a large difference in the prospect of gaining tenure or having job mobility when a position is not working out. Similarly, a guaranteed summer salary that provides time for your project is a real enticement.

Candidates sometimes overdo negotiating for more salary and benefits. Although the tangibles are very important and can make a huge difference to your research productivity, you must take some care not to have too much of a stake in the outcome of negotiations unless you are truly weighing competing offers. I have seen people talk themselves out of a job because they could not get what they wanted or thought they deserved. This is not a great idea unless you are genuinely dissatisfied and feel that you have alternatives. Do not always assume that the chair has great negotiating ability with the administration. In many cases, a sympathetic chair simply cannot squeeze more out of the dean or provost. In any event, it pays to be gracious in the long run; graciousness is a quality that I believe is much underappreciated in academia.

Earlier in this chapter, I considered the reasons for shifting to a nonacademic position for young PhDs who have always known or have come to realize that they do not have a sufficient taste for academic life. But what about those of you who either strike out in the job search or are unwilling to downgrade your expectations to accept an offer to an undesirable position? My advice to you is to try to hold on for at least one more job cycle.

A well-known scholar in my field and a former student of mine went on the job market as she was completing her PhD. She was able to get an interview in a leading department but had a terrible time with her job talk, because as soon as she commenced, she was besieged by questions and challenges. I can still remember the torrent of tears and self-recriminations as she related the experience to me when she returned. It was a sorry sight, but I did my best to reassure her that, in fact, her prospects would be much better if she finished her thesis and spent a year teaching and working on papers at Penn, a homemade postdoc of sorts. In fact, the very next year, after bulking up her curriculum vita and gaining some equanimity, she became one of the hot prospects on the market.

Going into a holding pattern is a wise strategy for a committed and capable recent PhD as long as you understand that you must take advantage of the waiting period between job cycles to get work done and, perhaps, gain teaching experience if you don't have it. It can make a big difference in your chances of success. Obviously, there are limits to this strategy: it depends on having a reasonable place to hang your hat while you work and wait. So, it makes sense to affiliate with a research center if your department cannot accommodate you during the gap.

I'm often asked whether a temporary teaching position, filling in while someone is on leave, is a good holding strategy. It depends on the quality of the post and the size of the teaching load that you will assume. If you are headed primarily for a teaching career, it can be a good option because you will gain experience and possibly exposure to other opportunities. And, in any event, a one-year position in a world of shifting chairs is better than sitting at home. However, if your aspirations are for a research-oriented university that gives high priority to publications, a full-time (six or, worse yet, eight courses a year) job may provide too little time to advance your publishing agenda. You are better off doing what you can to make ends meet while you hang out in a more visible research environment, even if it means staying in the department where you did your PhD. Your academic credentials and provenance convey a signal to future employers, like it or not. Climbing up in academia is always more difficult than moving laterally or taking a better job at a lower-prestige place.

In many respects, academia shares qualities with occupations like the arts, the entertainment world, and sports that are highly stratified and to which there are many more aspirants than good positions. Even before and certainly by the time that you leave graduate school, it is essential to take a clear-headed reading of your aspirations and what you are willing to settle for in the way of an academic job. This means testing the waters through a job search, reassessing your situation if need be, and then retesting the job market if you do not fare well the first time. After a second round, most trained and well-credentialed candidates will find an acceptable position, even if the job may not have fully fulfilled their initial aspirations. As I observed earlier, almost everyone moves from a better graduate department to a less prestigious place in their first teaching position. The issue of managing the first job and perhaps improving on it is the theme of the next chapter, about being an assistant professor.

3

BEING AN ASSISTANT PROFESSOR

In the various piles of articles and clippings amassed to prepare the chapters of this book, the largest by far concerned being an assistant professor. This is hardly surprising: few seasoned academics would disagree that the years between entering a full-time position and gaining tenure, or at least some measure of job security for academics in non-tenure teaching jobs, are usually the most challenging and stressful part of an academic career. I have read countless testimonies in the trade journals of how to manage—or, some would say, survive—the transition from graduate school or a postdoc to the first job and settling into an academic career. Much of what I will say in this chapter is applicable to readers both with and without tenure-track positions.

With the rapid shrinkage in the proportion of tenure-track positions and the growth of non-tenure full-time and part-time positions, I will devote some, but surely not enough, attention to the unique problems of the growing number of faculty who by choice or necessity are in positions that do not provide tenure. Still, the tenure process consumes an enormous amount of attention in the literature on higher education. But let me not jump ahead, the initial transition to academic life is the immediate concern of readers entering their first full-time position. This passage poses plenty of challenges of its own, long before the tenure process commences.

THE BEGINNING YEARS

Looking back on the experience of entering the profession, James Lang, who wrote a memoir about his experiences early in his career, remarks,

"Although sometimes I pine for the days of my youth, the one year of my life that I try to forget is my first year as a new faculty member."[1] He describes it as a year from hell. We academics may be too prone to self-reflection and too articulate in expressing our angst—overly dramatic, some might say—but after clearing the job-market hurdle and securing a suitable position, many young faculty members are incompletely prepared for the rigors of the first year.[2]

When you cross over from student to faculty member, it is not uncommon to revisit the feelings that many of you had on entering your doctoral program: self-doubt, confusion, uncertainty, and occasionally even dread. You are also likely to experience the counterbalancing feelings of excitement, of relief at finally having a chance to practice your trade, and at long last of being on the other side of the lectern. You have spent five to ten years learning how to be an academic; now you have a chance to actually be a professor. Yet many new assistant professors confess to the lurking feeling that they may not be up to the task of managing the welter of novel demands.

A first-year assistant professor recounts the following story that occurred in the first week of his appointment. Sensing that the new hire was feeling insecure, the chair of his department tried to reassure him of his worthiness for the position by telling him that he had earned his position and should just settle into the job. No sooner had the young man closed the door of his new office, the chair returned to give him a pile of papers that turned out to be the reviews of his job talk by his now-fellow colleagues. As he paged through the critical comments—some favorable, a few scathing—he began to question the motives of the chair and started wondering which of his colleagues might have found fault with his work. The mild bout of paranoia lingered as he began to encounter his colleagues over the next several weeks. Eventually, he decided to take the criticisms as a more benign reminder that he would do better as he acquired more experience.[3]

Entering a new role, even one that you have prepared for much of your life, is genuinely daunting. Most new faculty members begin their jobs with some experience from graduate school and part-time teaching or perhaps even more time in an adjunct position, but many still report that they were inadequately prepared for taking on the job of assistant professor. Surveys conducted on assistant professors' accounts of their early years have shown that a large proportion do not feel that their training adequately equipped them to contend with preparing for new classes, teaching and counseling students, advancing their research agenda, taking on the responsibilities of running a department, and the service demands often required of assistant professors.[4] Many also say that the expectations for tenure were unclear to them at the outset of their career.

It's sufficient to say that a large disconnect exists in academia between formal career training and doing the job. That is true for most professions, but the size of the gap between training and expected performance in academic life is compounded by the amount of scrutiny young academics are under—annual evaluations, reappointments often during the second year, and the tenure process for those on the tenure track. Only experience can fill the gap, which necessarily involves learning on the job. And learning on the job means dealing with uncertainty of how to meet a host of new expectations and obligations. The first part of this chapter is about how to learn the ropes and then make use of your newly acquired skills to build a record for reappointment and for tenure, if that is the next step in your career.

Among the most important skills you must acquire are balancing the competing demands from the workplace and the home front, gaining confidence in the classroom and learning to handle students successfully, acquiring diplomatic abilities to get along with your colleagues inside and outside the department, learning to say no when you really need to turn down a request for service or research collaboration, and building a network of professional friends and mentors who will help guide and support you through the early years of your career. I will also discuss how to sustain your research and writing in the early years of being an assistant professor.

READING THE DEPARTMENT CULTURE

In the beginning of an academic career, it helps to take careful stock of the academic culture of the department and the college or university that you have entered. Few job applicants have the luxury of getting to know that culture well before they enter it, mostly because the recruiting process typically is designed to reveal the most attractive features of the department while concealing its warts. It is not unlike courtship in former times, when couples often married without really knowing that much about each other. Marriage then was all about discovering just what couples had gotten themselves into.

In this sense, we share an experience akin to what professional anthropologists go through when they enter an unfamiliar culture. This happens to us in a less dramatic form when we move from one university to another or, an even bigger stretch, when we go from a university to a four-year or two-year college. To an outsider, the dissimilarities may appear superficial—a different campus or mix of students—but when you become an insider in a new institution, you quickly learn that many things operate quite differently from one locality to the next. Like anthropologists, we only get to know a new culture by living it, by learning the subtle assumptions, rules, understandings, and expectations. This happens by active participation and being gradually inducted into how things actually work in a department. Experienced hands will sometimes inform you, "That is not the way we do it here."

When I came to Penn, I had taught a class at Columbia as a graduate student, the same course (at least I thought) that I would teach in my new department. But on my first day in the office, I received a visit from a senior faculty member who had taught sections of the same course for years using his own textbook. Would I be using his textbook, he inquired of me. No, I replied, I planned to use a set of readings from different sources. He frowned and did not say another word except to tell me that the fraternities would probably not recommend my course because they had files of his previous exams and coached new students who entered his class. I had no idea from my prior experience that anything like this could occur. Needless to say, because I didn't use his textbook, this senior faculty member in my own field did not become my advocate or mentor over the next several years.

A well-traveled younger faculty member who held five positions over a period of eight years, largely owing to her family situation, wryly observes that there are certain commonalities to all the places that she worked. One of the key lessons she learned was that every department and larger administrative unit in which it is embedded has a distinctive political climate. Your job, she cautions, is to discover it.[5] The political culture of departments and universities is a good starting point for any discussion of becoming an assistant professor. The departmental culture has an immense influence on how younger faculty members feel about their new position and how readily they adjust to it.

New faculty members plunge into an existing organization system (a set of rules and understandings) and a culture (beliefs and expectations more or less shared by the members). Whether you will fit—or, for that matter, want to fit—into this micro-world is a question that you will be asking yourself from day one. Some of you will be saying to yourselves: "I am so lucky to be in a department that is such a pleasant place to work." And other readers may be asking, "How in the world did I ever end up here?" Most likely, many of you will have a mixed set of feelings about the academic culture that you have entered. You'll like some things about the way it works and wish that other things could be different.

Departments differ in certain familiar features that will be relevant to your own sense of well-being. Some are hierarchical in the way that decisions are made, whereas others are more equitable; departments vary in the degree to which members are collaborative or individualistic; they differ in the level of resources, both material and emotional, that they offer faculty, particularly new members; they tolerate or even promote varying levels of conflict and dissension; some are more broadly meritocratic in contrast to departments where rewards are doled out to political supporters; and the list of differences goes on and on. The important point is that the combination of features creates distinctive work milieus. Depending on their own predilections and needs, new faculty—in this case, you—will find them more or less congenial, supportive, and generative.

Like all small organizations, departments have institutional histories that appear to transcend even their present cast of characters and exist in settings that help reproduce their particular practices. I was trained in a notoriously dysfunctional graduate program at Columbia. Years later I was invited to participate in a formal review of the department where I was trained. Virtually no one who was a member when I was a graduate student remained on the faculty. Remarkably, though, by all accounts of the current faculty and students, the department retained much of its former culture. At the time, it was still rife with conflict at the faculty level, and many students felt unsupported. The culture survived even though a complete turnover in the faculty had occurred from the time I was there twenty-five years earlier.

The important point for you as a new member of this "family" is that you have to make sense and figure out how it works and how you are expected to fit into the picture. This knowledge may take some time and effort to acquire depending on how transparent, complex, or concealed departmental dealings are. One sure bet is that only rarely will your new colleagues completely share a conception of how things actually work. When there is this sort of consensus, you can get the lay of the land pretty quickly. More likely, though, it will take some time because you must sort through the differences in the accounts and actions of your colleagues. Your chair, let's say, tells you how the hiring practices work in your new department. Several weeks later, you get quite a different account from several of your new peers. Only later do you figure out that none of your informants rendered a view that fits your own experience. A familiar sociological mantra holds that a person's position in an organization shapes his or her perspective on the organization. Necessarily, there will be differences in perceptions of the departmental culture, but the magnitude of these differences will vary a lot in departments that work well or poorly.

It is important to keep in the back of your mind that all will not be revealed in the first several weeks or months on the job. Your first impressions may not be any more reliable than your initial impressions on entering a new country. It is helpful to examine what is written down in the form of handbooks, regulations, and department or university policies and compare that to faculty understandings of how things actually work. It may even be useful to jot down your observations at the beginning of your term in an informal diary or to keep a file of your e-mail observations to friends just to keep track of how your perceptions change over time (but be careful of recording these observations in public view, such as in a work e-mail account). The main point is that you will learn by doing, by immersing yourself in the daily routines of socializing with your colleagues, talking to staff, serving on departmental and university committees, and watching what happens at faculty meetings and seminars. If you are confused, don't be afraid to say so, but don't expect the confusion to lift until you have been in the department for a while. Your main job in the first year or two is to figure out how or whether you can fit in.

Most academics are accustomed to speaking their minds freely. Circumspection is not necessarily a trait selected for in academic life. I would never advise you to hold back your views about matters of substance and policy in your department, but it is wise to take your time and see how your own views align with the opinions of your colleagues. Being a well-respected colleague means that you are able to listen to and understand opinions that you might not share. You can count on one thing: your colleagues will have many different opinions than the ones you hold or those held at your previous institution. Whether it is about the stuff of your profession (theory, methods, leading controversies in the field) or about matters that impinge on your profession (tolerance for diversity, political differences, or ideas about how the department should work), you can be sure that in most places controversies will surface. The big difference among departments is how these controversies are handled and whether they will affect your future in that department. Being a successful colleague means having the ability to work with and get along with members of your department with whom you may not always agree. Of course, this is easier said than done.

In my early years at Penn, a well-known intellectual bully leaned hard on younger faculty to share his views about the discipline. He made my life miserable, as he did with most of his younger colleagues and many of his peers. This senior figure was so intolerable that I almost left Penn to avoid his scorn, contemptuousness, and sense of superiority. I've hardly ever met a more wretched human being, though he was a provocative and extremely able scholar. Believe it or not, I kept a toy punching bag in the cellar of my house so that I could exorcise my frustrations in the evenings after I had endured an encounter with him. The only satisfaction I ever got from being his colleague was when I eventually earned tenure, after which I was able to stand up to him in faculty meetings or when I witnessed him badgering a younger colleague.

Although there are not always bullies per se, academia is full of curmudgeonly colleagues who enjoy playing the devil's advocate. If you are smart, academia permits and even encourages a certain degree of intellectual independence. By and large, most departments do not even try to exclude disagreeable members so long as they have the right stuff when it comes to research and teaching. Some of these folks are really quite lovable; others are more like my former colleague—unpleasant and even antisocial. As a younger academic, you must work out how you will learn to live with difficult colleagues because you will inevitably encounter them in a department of more than five.

No doubt, responding to curmudgeons may be especially problematic for women, ethnic minorities, and gays as they, correctly or not, might enter a department feeling especially vulnerable to judgments of those who do not share the disadvantages of being in the minority. In the past several decades, we have built a structure in academia for dealing with persistently aggressive behavior directed at women and underrepresented minorities, especially if the behavior assumes a derogatory form. The problem, of course, is to distinguish between merely offensive behavior and behavior that crosses the line into bigotry or sexism. It is useful to keep a log of behaviors and to discuss the issue with trusted peers and mentors before using some of the legal protections against offensive behaviors. As for the rest, there is little to do but get a punching bag for your basement!

Sometimes these difficult characters are isolates and cause little trouble, but they can run in packs. Although we academics tend to be uninterested in holding positions of power, departments often can be torn apart when senior faculty are at war with one another or when a certain faction assumes dominance over their weaker colleagues. A few senior members who like to call the shots can easily control a department. If testimonies from accounts in the journals of higher education are any indication, one might conclude that this sort of factional conflict is more the rule than the exception. But I suspect, on the basis of broader and more representative surveys of academics about their daily lives, that protracted conflict occurs less often than one might think from reading the trade journals. In fact, the vast majority of assistant professors hold positive views of the level of support their departments provide and feel as though they made the right decision in selecting their first job.[6]

DEPARTMENTAL AND UNIVERSITY SERVICE

Governance in departmental matters is usually set by broader administrative guidelines. Deans select department chairs, who report to them, although typically the administration of a college or university relies on department recommendations. The influence of the chair in a given department varies tremendously depending on local traditions, faculty consent, and the chair's skills and interests. In some settings such as medical schools, the chair may hold tremendous power; in others, he or she is merely a facilitator with little or no power to effect policy without the consent of his or her colleagues. However, the chair will likely end up making assignments to fill committees within and outside the department. So depending on how things work in your department, your chair will probably ask you to participate on one or more committees inside or outside your home base.

Service is usually considered onerous and not infrequently viewed as a waste of time, but it is a necessary part of the housework of departments. Like housework, some members do it more willingly and graciously than others. A friend of mine and a scholar of great repute has always adopted the view that the best way to dodge these responsibilities is to demonstrate incompetence—also a common tactic among domestic partners! I don't agree. It does not serve you well to be careless about meeting your obligations or to be incompetent in performing them. Considerable resentment builds up against those who shirk their departmental and university responsibilities. Even when counterbalanced by other assets, inept colleagues, I suspect, take a toll on the collective sense of well-being.

The problem is that many younger faculty members, especially those on a tenure track, do not understand that although service to the department is always welcomed and appreciated, it is rarely significantly rewarded. Or perhaps it is better to say that it simply does not count very much toward building a record of accomplishment in a research-oriented university. The same is *not* true in community colleges and many four-year institutions, where it may well count for more than it does when tenure is involved or job security is at issue. It is important that you take careful stock, even in the first and second years of your appointment, of what service can do for you in your institution.

There are some real benefits for you: You get to know your colleagues and see them in action; you learn how things really work and may even be able to push them in a positive direction; you gain experience and build confidence in areas that could be important to you later in your career; and your efficacy and goodwill may translate into faculty support for remaining in your department should you choose to do so. At the university or college level, you make contacts, gain information, and possibly build support for your presence on campus. Moreover, believe it or not, some faculty members find contributing to the collective good inherently satisfying.

However, service on faculty committees can take a lot of time, and time is among the most precious assets you have as a younger faculty member. You must take some care that the hours you devote to committees do not detract too heavily from your teaching, scholarship, or family responsibilities and life outside of work. If you are adept at managing administrative responsibilities (as my friend recognized), you are likely to be invited to do more of them. And if you find that they give you a sense of competence that is not so easily gained from research and teaching, beware: you run some risk of specializing in what you are good at, but this is often held against you later. Of course, it is possible that the experience you gain will come in handy if you eventually decide that academic life, at least full-time academic life, is not for you.

The delicate question, one that almost all younger faculty face, is how to decline requests to do more service and administration. There's no standard etiquette for new faculty saying no to colleagues or the administration. In the best of circumstances, department policy and senior faculty are looking out for your interests and shielding you from an excessive amount of service demands. In the worse of circumstances, departments and senior faculty exploit their weakest members, inappropriately shucking off time-consuming tasks to the individuals who feel that they cannot afford to say no. In many instances, senior faculty and administrative figures are simply oblivious.

As a rule of thumb, you should not spend more than a day per week on service to your department and university, and you should probably do less if you can manage to do so in the first several years as an assistant professor at a university where research productivity counts heavily in your performance reviews. I would include in that total service to the profession, such as serving on a committee, holding an elected position, or having an editorial job in your professional associations, which can also gobble up a lot of your time. Of course, if you can get release time from teaching for your committee work, that is another matter altogether, but most young faculty do not have that option. I favor a direct approach in responding to requests: "I'm not sure it's wise for me to agree to join the committee on increasing diversity on the campus. I'm already spending half a day per week on admissions and almost that much time on our institutional review board. I'm afraid that doing more will take away from completing my book before my tenure review. I'm sure that I'll be able to take on more service when my book is off to the publisher." That sort of response will usually be enough for a reasonable department chair or university dean. If it is not, then you will have to decide whether it is better to accept more service or not, depending on the circumstances, which is not an easy decision.

My point is not that you should resist doing campus or professional service. Service work can be a good investment of your time, and departments appreciate young faculty who share the load and reach out on campus and in the community. It is just that you must take care not to let these roles crowd out your time for teaching, research, and writing while you are an assistant professor, unless your institution clearly counts these tasks in the assessment of your performance. At most research-oriented universities and colleges, they count for relatively little in a tenure review.

Again, it is often women and underrepresented minorities who find themselves vulnerable to requests to help serve on this or that committee, especially because they are susceptible to claims that they are needed to provide diverse perspectives. That is all to the good unless these same people find themselves overloaded by responsibilities that are not counted when the time of reckoning occurs. So beware not to get sucked into so many committee responsibilities that you have insufficient time for the part of your job that matters most for your long-term prospects—teaching and research.

HANDLING YOUR TEACHING LOAD

There are some unpleasant facts in life, such as when you get older, your metabolism slows down and you can't afford to eat as much as you used to without gaining weight. So, too, it also seems grossly unfair that teaching loads generally increase as you descend the academic prestige ladder. Presumably, at the lower rungs of the ladder, there are also lower expectations for publishing, but that is far from true universally. Most second- and third-tier research universities and the majority of four-year institutions seem to expect you to do it all. In any event, a two-course load per semester, or five per trimester, is still fairly standard in most top-quality universities and leading departments for most disciplines. The variations are enormous from place to place and department to department within a given university, but few have the luxury of a one-course per semester load. In the majority of institutions, the teaching load is more likely to be three courses a semester and even higher at lower-ranked institutions with limited resources and that are primarily devoted to teaching.

Young academics, and even mature ones, must become adept at handling the competing demands of performance both inside and outside of the classroom while preserving time for your research agenda, especially for getting your work in print. The issue of time management that came up in the previous chapters now reemerges in full form at this early stage in your academic career. There simply are not enough hours in the day to do a really first-rate job if you are truly conscientious about all the demands you must handle.

Many young academics enter their first job with some teaching experience under their belt; however, a large number have taught only a course or two during their graduate years and perhaps during a postdoc or a temporary appointment. In rapid fashion, you may be required to teach two or three, possibly four, different courses, many of which you have not prepared for before you begin your appointment.

That is why I suggested in the previous chapter that you seriously consider the institutional demands for teaching in guiding your job search. But let's assume that you did, and the best job you could find requires a 3/3 teaching load (three classes each semester). Perhaps this requirement has been softened by the fact that you have only two new class preparations, one each semester, but things could be worse and you may be expected to do two new preparations each semester. How can you possibly manage this and still preserve time for research?

There is an easy, if not satisfying, answer to this question. The fact is that some people can do it and others cannot, and many academic institutions often adopt a sink-or-swim attitude toward new faculty. I hope this is not the case for you, but I'm going to assume that it is. Here are some tips for managing the crush of teaching responsibilities.

First, draw liberally from the numerous sources that are now online or in disciplinary publications aimed at providing syllabi and course materials. Although the course should obviously reflect your interests and have your own imprint, if only because it makes your classes more stimulating and effective, there's a lot of good help available for course preparation. Feel free to borrow from colleagues and peers inside and outside your department. Most faculty members are happy to share their course lists and recommend texts or readers that may be effective teaching aids. Don't feel that you must create your own list from scratch when you teach a new course, though you certainly will want to put your own distinctive mark on it.

There is an established etiquette for drawing from the work of others. Always give credit if you borrow from someone else's reading list. It doesn't hurt you, and it may help them. In any case, they will appreciate it. You can do that by noting on your course list, "I have benefited from the suggestions of . . . ," or just write helpful sources a note of thanks. Never be reluctant to acknowledge help received.

Second, I hate to say this, but don't belabor the task of constructing a syllabus or choosing texts. It is great when you get the right intellectual balance in your course the first time you teach it, but this will inevitably happen through trial and error. I've always added new materials each year, some of which I've only read in a cursory fashion, because it spices up the course for me. If these materials don't work well, you can drop them the next time. Use your students' response to the readings or textbook each year to readjust; they will generally welcome the opportunity to give feedback. Your course syllabus is always a work in progress.

Keep your preparation time to a manageable amount. Recently, one of my graduate students who was teaching an introductory course in the department told me that she had decided not to seek a teaching job because she could not even imagine the time that it would take. "How much time are you spending on your course?" I asked. "About fifty to sixty hours a week," she replied. "I couldn't do it in less." Well, the fact is that her impossible standards for herself were driving her crazy. In the beginning, you will probably need to devote a lot of time to teaching, but it should not be a full-time job unless it involves more than two preparations. It is probably reasonable to spend two days per class on preparation and course obligations the first time you offer a course, but after that you may be able to shave it down to one and a half days a week per course. Some people will do a little less and some a little more depending on class size and whether they have assistance in grading.

I found teaching in the beginning of my career difficult because of my chronic apprehension about my performance in the classroom. Classes usually went well, but I worried excessively about being underprepared and was often preoccupied by these anxieties. So my solution was to be overprepared. I read a lot of background material that never got into my lectures, and I still feared that I wouldn't be able to answer some bright undergraduate's question. If you share these anxieties, you must start the difficult process of abandoning them. You know a lot more about your subject than your students, and if you don't on occasion, then welcome their contributions. The problem is that you cannot afford to be both occupied and preoccupied with your teaching obligations. For many of us, it takes a while to get the hang of being an effective teacher, whether you are lecturing or, if you are fortunate enough, teaching a small seminar. Almost everyone gets better over time: more confident, more relaxed, and more skilled in presenting materials effectively so long as they continue to do a reasonable amount of preparation.

Years ago graduate students were thrown into teaching without any instruction or training. Things are different now. Most graduate programs offer classes on teaching. If you never participated in one, many campuses now offer opportunities to beginning and even mature faculty to benefit from advice in course organization and teaching techniques. Avail yourselves of these aids because teaching is a craft that you can learn with good supervision. Naturally, some academics take to teaching more easily than others, but we all can profit from help and almost all of us gain from classroom experience.

Students love attention and nurturance, and why shouldn't they? Providing it can take almost as much time as structuring a course, teaching the class, and grading. It is often quite gratifying to chat with students who come into your office. You receive valuable feedback from their responses to the course, enjoy getting to know them, and can sometimes play a prominent role in their intellectual and personal development. But unless you are at an institution where your main responsibilities and rewards are linked to teaching, you must set some limits on the time you spend with students outside the classroom. Otherwise, students could consume all your waking hours. So factor in ample time for office hours and perhaps an occasional lunch or coffee, but you must devise ways of preserving time for your research, writing, and other professional obligations, especially in the beginning of your career.

Some useful tactics may be to restrict your office hours to certain times of the day or, perhaps, to explain to students that you reserve your morning hours, as I do, for research and writing. A lot of queries and even feedback on assignments can and should occur by e-mail, though there is no good substitute for face-to-face appointments.

One of the most difficult teaching problems that young faculty face is dealing with students who require a lot of extra academic help or, more commonly, who face a serious personal or family crisis and seek your help. Or perhaps a student is behaving inappropriately in class or has cheated on an exam. Suddenly, you find yourself in a situation where a single student requires an inordinate amount of your time, crowding out hours that you allocated for teaching preparation or research. If this happens to you, I suggest seeking help from your chair, relevant colleagues, or appropriate administrative personnel who are specifically trained to deal with these sorts of student issues. Of course, you must be prepared to help out, but try not to be drawn into the problem more than is necessary. Understandably, your first response may be to offer advice and assistance that often goes beyond your training or competency. You and the student may be better off if you can make a good referral to a place on campus staffed by experts in remediation, counseling, or financial advice. In other words, don't be a therapist, parent, or friend to your students. Doing so can often ill serve you and your students. If I sound a bit hard-hearted, let me assure you that my advice comes from learning that on balance it is better to recognize the limits of your role than to exceed them.

Managing to set limits on your time with both undergraduates and graduate students, should you be teaching in a program that offers an advanced degree, is frequently more difficult for women than men. Unfairly, students expect women to be more nurturing, patient, and generous with their time and therefore tend to rely on them more. Male faculty members may find it easier than female faculty members to say no to a student requiring lots of help or perhaps even a student in need. This puts women in a bit of a bind because they may be inclined to give more than they reasonably should. What to do about this difference associated with gender? In the best case, it should become part of the dialogue of the department, but it is sometimes hard to bring up this discrepancy, especially for female assistant professors outnumbered by older, senior male colleagues. You can sometimes get assistance from a sympathetic senior colleague, chair, or even a figure in the administration in helping you work out a good balance in consulting your students.

In graduate programs, the problem of time can become more acute if you find working with too many doctoral students to be more of a chore than a pleasure (although sometimes it can be both). Even as a senior professor who takes great pleasure in mentoring graduate students, I found that I had to set a limit on the number of dissertations that I supervised. This means occasionally turning away students whom you might otherwise work with if your load were not so great. As a junior faculty member, it is critical not to overcommit to serving on dissertation committees. It is stimulating and gratifying to work with graduate students, but it is also extremely time-consuming and a job for which you cannot cut too many corners. Start by serving on a committee or two but avoid chairing dissertations, if you can, at least until you get your professional footing. You can plead inexperience in the first year or two of an appointment. I strongly advise against taking on a large load of doctoral supervision at the outset of your career unless you are certain that you can handle it and the many other obligations that are part of your job.

Graduate students understandably gravitate to faculty members who give them a lot of time. In almost every department, there are inevitably faculty members whose reputation is that they are poor mentors because they are excessively demanding, exploitative in collaborations, prone to procrastination when given chapters to read, or merely going through the motions of supervision but providing little actual assistance. You definitely don't want to be one of those people, but you also must exercise some discretion in the other direction as well, at least when you are in the early stages of your career. If your senior colleagues are ungenerous in the help that they offer graduate students, it is important that you not pick up their workload entirely at the expense of your future. Figure out how many dissertation committees you can handle, given your existing time commitments, and stay within that limit. Again, if need be, talk the matter over with senior colleagues whose opinions you trust.

HOW TO DEVELOP THE HABIT OF RESEARCH AND WRITING

For those of you in research-oriented universities and colleges or departments looking to build their national reputations, your jobs require competent teaching and service, but your research grants and publications will weigh heavily on your future prospects in the department. If you are not in such a place but hope to move to one in the future, your record of research productivity is no less critical to your chances of success. And, for some of you, research may count for less in your job than teaching or service, but it may still be an important part of your motivation for entering academia and an essential part of your professional well-being. This section of the chapter is especially for you.

Okay, one day for service, three or four days for teaching; how does a young faculty member ever accomplish research and writing when you are already committed to a full-time job just to keep your head above water? It is not easy, but you can manage it. Indeed, you have to learn how to do so in the early years of your career, or it will probably never happen. It is essential to incorporate the habit of scholarly research into your daily routine, and especially the habit of writing and publishing your findings.

Let me start with another cruel fact: most of you simply cannot afford to relegate research and writing just to the summers and an occasional sabbatical, if you are indeed fortunate enough to receive one as an assistant professor. This approach might work if you only need a handful of publications following your appointment to earn a permanent place in your department. But I suspect that this is not true for the majority of readers, who are or who want to be on a tenure track in a research-oriented institution. More likely, you need to produce at least a greatly modified version of your thesis in book form and/or a number of published articles.

Younger academics ask me all the time about how much is enough to earn tenure if they are in a tenure-track job or seeking a tenure-track appointment. The answer varies greatly by discipline and department. In other words, disciplinary standards between chemistry, economics, and French literature vary so widely that any general figure I could provide would be misleading; moreover within each of these disciplines, there is far more variability from department to department in a university or even a college than across the disciplines. About one thing we can be sure: whatever requirements existed ten years ago may not be true today. There has been by all accounts considerable inflation in tenure standards over the past decade or two.

I am going to assume—and it is a fairly safe assumption for those of you on the tenure track—that whatever the disciplinary and local standards are, you will be hard-pressed to meet them by doing research and writing only three months a year in the summer. Therefore, you need to carve out time during the academic year to research and write while you are teaching. How do you find hours during the day or on weekends to advance your scholarly agenda when you are preparing for your courses, teaching, tending to your students, and serving on committees? There are many books, articles, advice columns, and blogs that attempt to answer this question, but I will give you my own take on how to safeguard time for your writing and how to make good use of the hours that you set aside.

First and most important is to arrange room in your schedule so that you can devote some time every day or, at least, most days to scholarship and writing. It may be first thing in the morning or last thing at night, but you need to develop a routine much as people do when they exercise regularly. Protect that space in your day because it will enable you to get a remarkable amount done over time if it becomes part of your workday routine. You may be saying to yourself that it is impossible to find time to do this, and it might be true. If that is the case, you must be forewarned that you are probably going to face problems in building a record of scholarly accomplishment or productivity.

Most assistant professors can do it if they are committed to the idea and reasonably disciplined about implementing a schedule. Three hours a day, five days a week, will get you pretty far along if you are moderately efficient in using the time to do your planning, reading and research, and analysis and writing. I understand that this may involve different chunks of time in different disciplines whether you are in the library, the lab, or the field. Still, sticking to routines helps a lot in moving your research agenda along.

The next issue is how to use your time efficiently. Most of us are not blessed with efficient work habits at the beginning of our academic careers. I certainly was not when I started out. How well I remember when early in my career I went off one summer to the woods by a lake to write! It seemed so idyllic, but I spent weeks in front of a typewriter every day trying to write a single paper. I discovered that I brought with me an expert critic; no sooner than I began to put something down on paper, this critic found problems with each sentence that I drafted. I knew that this was an impossible way to work, but I could not stop censuring myself. It was a depressing display of the affliction that ails many young academics. We have internalized many of the criticisms of our teachers and seem incapable of putting them aside as we work. It took me several years of writing before I became more adept at censoring my censor.

I discovered that I could not write and edit at the same time. It was like driving a car while pushing on the accelerator and the brake more or less simultaneously. It simply didn't get me very far. Gradually I learned how to relax into writing, much as with practice and in time you learn to acquire any skill. You must allow the writing to flow without an undue amount of consciousness. The editing can come later as you review what you've written, but cut yourself some slack in the beginning and just try to put your ideas, argument, or data description down in a very rough draft. You can always clean up the text either the next day when you start writing (as I like to do), or after you have a first draft completed. I can almost guarantee that if you write regularly, it will become notably easier to do over time. It may even become fun, as it eventually did for me.

So unrelenting was my criticism in the beginning that I had to convince myself that I was only writing a "report," not a book, when I faced the challenge of writing up my first major research project. When I cleaned up the "report" a bit, I sent it out to several trusted colleagues, and they told me that I had written a book that needed very little work before it could be published. So I learned slowly and painfully to trust my professional competence. Some young academics have difficulty believing at the beginning of their academic careers that they have the authority to practice their craft. With experience, this sense of authority grows and becomes more deeply internalized. Once it does, you will find that it is much easier to write without the critic inside constantly harping on the inadequacies of your ideas, argument, or presentation of evidence.

CIRCULATING YOUR WORK

Perfectionism is the enemy of productivity in academia. Over the years, I've seen a number of very smart people fail in academia simply because they could not stand to let go of their work before it was finished to their ultimate satisfaction, and they were never satisfied enough with their drafts to share them with colleagues, much less reviewers. If this description fits you, you'd better rethink what you are doing. Your scholarly work cannot have an impact if nobody ever reads or criticizes it. So the real question is when to circulate it and to whom?

Not the first draft, and possibly not the second, but certainly by draft number three it is time to share your work with a peer or even a mentor. There is likely to be no time, even after draft six, when you cannot find a lot to criticize in your own research and writing. Be prepared to get feedback as soon as you feel you have a "working draft." A working draft means that you still have changes to make or sections to add, but you have developed the main argument or set of results coherently enough that readers will be able to provide useful input. This process, of course, may work differently according to your academic discipline. In the sciences, the process of writing up the results in ways that will satisfy reviewers, while important, can be less of an onerous task than producing the data.

Writing groups of junior faculty who exchange drafts are an excellent way to begin the process of getting feedback. Peers can be kind and sympathetic and can also suggest ways of strengthening the text before you pass it along to a mentor. I would ordinarily suggest waiting to show a mentor a slightly more developed draft. Sometimes, if you have received positive feedback through these stages, it is appropriate and strategically wise to send your work out to one or more experts in your field who may take special interest in your ideas, argument, or findings. Some fields have venues for circulating drafts and eliciting comments as a working paper. And, of course, many papers get presented in small or larger conferences that provide critical feedback on work in process.

Mentors can also help in suggesting readers for a fairly finished product. I frequently advise my younger colleagues and collaborators to send a paper in draft form to a senior professional friend or acquaintance who might have an interest in their topic. This accomplishes two things simultaneously. First, you get another pair of eyes to look over the paper before you submit it to a journal for formal review. And, second, if the outsider likes your work, it may prompt a letter of support later on when you are up for promotion. I don't, however, advise a mass mailing to anyone and everyone who might have an interest in the topic. It will not prompt much response and could cause irritation.

Here is a rule of thumb about writing. If you aren't circulating papers or chapters of a book during the first year of your appointment, you should pick up the pace. If little or nothing is happening by your second year, seek some help, because you are going to need it if you are at a research university or college that requires scholarly publication for tenure. The idea, at least in the social sciences, is to keep a number of things in the pipeline for publication at the same time. You are submitting a paper for publication or revising a text that has already been reviewed at the same time that you are circulating an early draft of a new paper and, if possible, beginning to draft a third one. You may need to modify this approach if you are working on a book, but the same idea applies to chapters as to papers. You must learn to keep several balls in the air at the same time if you are to have a good flow of scholarly work.

Some people learn to develop this pipeline of production in graduate school and get better at it if they are fortunate enough to have a postdoctoral position. However, many academics go directly from graduate school to their first job and must become more adept at this kind of multitasking. As I've said, writing becomes easier the more you do it, so experience is the best way to become more productive. Your department will certainly monitor your progress, but it is far better if you manage it more actively by setting out your writing goals and adhering to your schedule. Of course, there will be slippage; it is very rare that someone tells me that they did more in a semester or summer than they expected to accomplish. It usually works the other way around, so allow for slippage in your schedule, especially in the first several years of your career.

WHERE TO PUBLISH

Younger scholars often have questions about where to publish. Unless it is obvious, consult with knowledgeable colleagues or mentors before you submit an article or book manuscript. Of course you want to publish in the best-ranked journals or with a good press, but it is not always possible to do so. The question of how far down to go in publication outlets is a difficult one. Early in your career, you can usually afford to publish in a weaker journal or press, even if you are in a department that puts a high premium on the top outlets. But if you are in a top-tier or second-tier university, you must take some care about the placement of your work because it will likely matter. It is important to place at least some of your work in the more prestigious journals or with a good press if you are producing a book.

As online journals are growing by leaps and bounds, take some care not to publish promiscuously in online journals that have little or no credibility because it could come back to haunt you. In many disciplines, chapters in edited books are regarded as vita stuffers: that is, they are often dismissed as "real" publications because they have not gone through independent peer review. This may or may not be fair, but unfortunately you may face the situation where your work is summarily dismissed later on if it appears primarily in book chapters. Again, local standards in how your work will be assessed prevail, but you should exercise discretion in where you publish if you want to have the flexibility to move later on.

This probably means that you should reach as high as you can in the publication outlet, understanding that you may receive more rejections as a result. But the benefit is that you will get good criticism, often from anonymous reviewers along the way. It sometimes hurts, but it is often helpful to have the weaknesses of your argument, data, or analysis pointed out. At the same time, you will occasionally get inane or outright inaccurate readings of your work. If this happens, you can occasionally appeal to an editor. It is usually best to ignore the advice and submit your work elsewhere. It is not worth spending a lot of time protesting the unfairness of reviews unless you are absolutely certain that a review has done your work a great disservice and your appeal has a reasonable prospect of succeeding. Otherwise you will be wasting your time.

It is exceedingly rare, at least in the social sciences, to have an article or book accepted without revision. Far more typically, you will receive an R&R—that is, revise and resubmit. This is an encouraging response. Do not respond too quickly or too slowly when you get an R&R. A very rapid response is not recommended unless the changes called for are merely cosmetic; a very quick turnaround to an R&R could signal that you are paying too little attention to the reviewers. However, a very slow response runs the risk that the resubmitted piece will go out to a different set of reviewers who may have other criticisms of your work, a likely event since it is part of the reviewers' job to find weaknesses in your argument, data, or analysis and interpretation. Always treat the reviewers' comments with respect and respond explicitly to them in a letter that details the changes you have made in response to their concerns. Keep in mind that you don't always have to accept their criticisms, but it is wise to acknowledge them and explain why you are not heeding their advice.

I mentioned the necessity of entrepreneurship in academia in the previous chapter, but you must take some care at putting it into practice in your early years. More and more universities at all levels provide internal funding to write grant proposals. It is worthwhile to undertake in your early years, assuming that you have a reasonable shot at funding. I recommend looking at the successful proposals in your institution as a good place to start. The task of writing a grant proposal can be professional stimulating and, of course, rewarding if you are funded, but it is often quite time-consuming unless the funding program is primarily designed for fledging scholars. So be sure not to get yourself into a situation where you are writing proposals *instead of* professional papers.

If you are seeking federal funding, you can be virtually certain that a successful research grant will require a great deal of time. Research proposals to the government only rarely are funded on the first submission. My advice is only to undertake this sort of effort in collaboration with more experienced hands, for example, with colleagues who have previously written successful grant proposals. It is a great learning experience to work with a team of researchers on a proposal, but you must take care not to invest too much time in this sort of activity at the very beginning of your career. In addition, before you agree to join a team, be certain that you will be protected by colleagues if and when the grant comes through—specifically, that you will have time and money to publish from the project if the grant is approved. In the following chapter, I lay out some rules for junior/senior collaboration that you might want to consult.

EXPANDING YOUR PROFESSIONAL NETWORK

Earning job security is all about gaining the positive regard of your colleagues and the administration of your university or college. At community colleges and university programs that primarily serve undergraduates, being a good teacher and a valued member of your department may be sufficient to earn your reappointment and perhaps a permanent position, albeit one that does not always come with tenure. Institutions with a tenure track ordinarily look for a strong record of scholarly publication and professional recognition, though many institutions less well endowed with research programs will often want some evidence of scholarship and place more emphasis on teaching and service. The more distinguished the institution, the more that professional reputation outside your department counts for your long-term prospects. Your scholarly work and output were probably why they hired you, and these will surely be the major reasons they will ask you to stay.

Getting your work into published form is the main way that you gain professional recognition, but it is certainly not the only way. You must try to build a professional network that acknowledges and uses your scholarly work or findings. These days the Internet and even social media can play an important part in circulating your work. Most universities now try to publicize the work of their faculty in press releases and newsletters. Like it or not, it is hard to ignore the benefits of having your grants, books, papers, and awards acknowledged locally and nationally. This information can put you in touch with interested colleagues at your institution, in the rest of the country, and abroad. It often garners invitations to conferences and colloquia at other universities, helps with soliciting research grants, and enhances the reception of high-quality research and scholarship. Needless to say, it helps very little when the work is mediocre.

There is an awful lot of work getting published in journals and books. The question of how and why it gets recognized, cited, and appreciated is the topic of many a study in the sociology of science and the sociology of knowledge. Some academics are understandably reluctant to toot their own horns. It may appear unseemly, self-interested, and, at least in our fantasies, unnecessary because good work should attract attention by itself. But without putting too fine a point on it, information travels most rapidly through social and professional networks and public venues such as newspapers and other mass media. It is therefore useful for you to consider how you can enter these networks of information.

At the beginning of your career, the process of attracting professional attention is often painfully slow. Many years ago, a now-prominent member of my department asked me how to get invitations to smaller meetings and conferences. My advice: The most important step you can take is to get your work out and into print. If you do good work, it will probably receive recognition. But I told him that it is perfectly acceptable, indeed even desirable, to send your published papers to central people in your field who have a direct interest in the scholarship that you are doing. These days it is simple because you can easily attach it to an e-mail. As I said earlier, I would not recommend mass mailings, but try to target your communications to people who really might want to read your paper because it relates to their ongoing work. If a mentor or colleague offers to send it out for you, this is preferable, if only because it feels less self-serving.

I've often asked newly minted PhDs whether they have remained in touch with their doctoral advisors after completing their degree. It is remarkable how few young academics take the time to send papers to their advisors or even merely keep them up-to-date on their whereabouts. Perhaps they feel it would be a bother or even impolite to write from time to time, but this is usually not the case. Most senior academics, if they are worth their salt, value these communications from their professional offspring. Similarly, it is important to reach out to more senior figures in your field after you meet them at conferences and academic meetings. This practice is not arrogant or self-aggrandizing but proper professional protocol for young academics.

ACADEMIC MEETINGS AND CONFERENCES

You build networks in part by going to professional meetings and especially smaller conferences that may or may not be by invitation only. Presenting papers or contributing to poster sessions at professional conferences is de rigueur in academic life. Many young academics enjoy conferences: you see friends, meet new people, and, most importantly, find out what is going on in your field. When I was starting out, professional conferences were smaller, and it was easier to make contact with senior figures in my field. As the size of professional associations has grown, they have become a little more unwieldy, but they are still the major forums for getting to know others in your field.

The best approach is to meet people in action, when you are presenting a paper at a professional conference. Try to take advantage of these occasions to seek out your colleagues from other institutions. Your former graduate-school peers often provide an easy conduit for cross-department contact. But don't be shy about asking to have coffee with someone that you do not know, even a senior scholar whose work has been influential to you. It is standard practice to write in advance of professional conferences and ask for a bit of time to consult. Expect that you will sometimes be rejected. Professor X or Y will be there but only for a couple of hours and may not have time to meet you. Not every senior figure is equally generous or receptive to these sorts of requests, but you will be amazed at how many senior academics are if you have good intellectual reasons for seeking them out.

Actively participating in professional meetings and reaching out to peers and senior scholars in other departments come with certain reciprocal obligations on your part. It almost goes without saying that the least you can do is show graciousness and appreciation for the time others volunteer, and this is probably sufficient. You build a lot of obligations from the favors that others do for you over time. I will come back to this topic in the next chapter because these obligations require reciprocity on your part, but the reciprocity may not always come in the form of tit for tat. Indeed, the dealings of junior and senior faculty rarely have this quality, especially when they are in different departments. The advice, assistance, and sponsorship typically flow downward. You will have your turn to be primarily on the giving end when you become a senior academic.

Problems can arise when you overtax or demand too much in this exchange. As a junior scholar, you must take care to recognize the invisible line between asking for help (or being offered it) and putting too much of a load on professional colleagues, either senior or junior. Be judicious and sensitive in your requests so that you do not exploit colleagues who might otherwise take an interest in your professional development. From my own experience, I've found that few younger scholars err on the side of asking too much, but you certainly don't want to be regarded as someone who does. It damages the most precious asset you have as an academic: your reputation.

REAPPOINTMENT AND THE ROAD TO TENURE
(OR JOB SECURITY)

Most tenure-track appointments are for three years, whereas adjunct teaching posts and non-tenure-track positions may require annual renewal of the contract. Typically, annual reviews look at teaching, service, and good relations with colleagues and students, although signs of scholarly production may also be assessed. At a three-year review, you can be pretty certain that publication will count, although some departments are more tolerant of a slow start than others. The point is that you must know the standards and be prepared to satisfy them.

Surveys of young academics suggest that those on a tenure track are likely to learn expectations for tenure fairly soon and typically understand how the system works by their second or third year.[7] However, the process of reappointment for a tenure-track position usually starts by the second year, since faculty normally receive at least a year's notice if their contract is not going to be renewed. In any event, most departments these days provide annual feedback even if you have a three-year appointment. Most junior faculty members know where they stand, at least in a general sense, almost from the start. Yet there is still a lot of room for ambiguity in interpreting these job evaluations, even if you receive annual written reviews. Faculty not on the tenure track may be more at the mercy of the economic health of their institution, and earning job security may involve making yourself indispensable in teaching and service.

Reading the tea leaves about the future can require some imagination because they typically come in the form of somewhat vague statements: "You need to publish more in top-tier journals during the next few years." "Your teaching of undergraduates is above average, but your contact with graduate students has been limited." And so on. Reviews necessarily are directed to improvements that you could or should make, but they are rarely so specific that you can simply check them off a list when you make adjustments in your performance. It helps to have explicit conversations with your chair and other senior members of your department to get as much feedback as possible. At the same time, you don't want to display too much anxiety or insecurity by asking for reassurance when it might not be forthcoming—yet another fine line that you must learn to walk.

Many departments now appoint senior mentors for younger faculty to provide advice and feedback on your performance, which supplements what you receive from the chair or a designated person on the personnel committee that handles your review or reappointment. If this person provides inadequate advice and feedback, I suggest finding a colleague in the department whom you trust to serve as a confidant. Pick this person carefully because he or she can be an invaluable source of information and an ally. It should be someone who is well regarded in the department and who is willing and able to be candid in their communication to you. It doesn't help merely to be told what you would like to hear.

Reappointment comes very early in the tenure process, but it can be a harbinger of things to come. If you are a close call, you must take serious stock of whether you are at the right place. A positive evaluation provides some breathing space for the next three years, but you should never assume too much on the basis of an initial positive review. It is a good time to ask yourself whether you need to make some mid-course corrections in teaching, service, and, of course, your program of research. This is another point when young academics, even those on a tenure track, may rethink whether they are well suited to academia or should be considering a transition to a non-academic job.

Although dropping out of academia may feel like a failure to some, for others the decision to leave full-time teaching can be liberating. Some young people move into administrative posts with opportunities to teach part-time; others go into business, government, or social service when they realize that their PhD can lead to good alternatives to an unrewarding academic job. Take your reappointment as a point of reappraisal and not necessarily as a reason to continue even though you are renewed, unless you are feeling a reasonable measure of contentment. Although most young academics are able to pick up the pace in the second term of their assistant professorship, this is far more likely to happen if you enjoy what you do. If you do not, you must begin to think about alternatives while you have ample time to pursue them.

A lot of job movement takes place among assistant professors. Assistant professors not on a tenure track often try to find a position that provides more stability. Typically, they do so by publishing and earning positive teaching ratings. I could find very little systematic data about how often this actually occurs. Although it is widely known that tenured positions are declining as a fraction of all academic jobs, it is less clear how many people start out in a non-tenured position and work their way into a tenured post. Judging from the trade journals, it happens not infrequently, but I could find few statistics based on longitudinal surveys that follow PhDs over time or even many general studies on the time to tenure.[8]

The more successful you are, the more you are likely to think about moving to a more desirable department if you are discontented with your initial appointment. Making a move involves mobilizing your network at a fairly early stage in your career. Listen to your mentors' advice about whether a move is wise. Recently, a student of mine expressed great disenchantment in the second year of her appointment, even though she was confident about getting reappointed. She was understimulated and lacked close colleagues. However, she was at a good university and the prospects of moving elsewhere were far from certain. I advised her to wait another year before going on the market. A year later she reported being much happier and more integrated into the department and university, though she still expected to relocate in the long term. Of course, this doesn't always happen, but unless you are very sure that your current position is not going to work out, I would suggest waiting until the third or fourth year before embarking on a serious job search. It is quite a different matter if another department encourages or invites you to apply.

Applying to other, and presumably better or more suitable, departments often has ramifications for your standing in your current position. Your colleagues can take it as a sign of "disloyalty" that prompts a negative reaction; occasionally it improves your internal standing, especially if an attractive department invites you to apply. Never assume that you can keep negotiations with other departments completely a secret. Academics are terrible gossips, and word about who is applying and being considered for different positions is part of the currency exchanged at meetings and in electronic communications. I almost always advise telling your department chair or a senior colleague that you are looking elsewhere. You may get a more sympathetic response from your department if you can couch your search as a personal decision, as in fact it often is: "My partner is unhappy," "My ex is moving with the children," "I need to be in an urban environment," and so on. Your colleagues, even if they do not resent your looking around for a different position, need to understand why you might want or need to leave.

In fact, switching departments is a common fact of academic life. Very few faculty members stay in the same place their entire academic careers, so you need not feel that a move is akin to a divorce. It is not. Nonetheless, it is not always true that a change represents an improvement. You will be far more aware of the limitations of your current department than of some other place, so take some care to assure yourself that you are not "out of the frying pan and into the fire." It happens all the time, and there are transaction costs to being an academic vagabond.

THE TENURE PROCESS

The struggle for tenure is the stuff of legend in academic circles. I only learned that I received tenure on the day before I would have been out of a job. My story is not even worth recounting, although it was full of drama and intrigue at the time. It is part of the narrative of struggle that structures the early phase of many academic careers. Few people make the transition from assistant professor to associate professor with ease. If our journals of higher education are any indication, it is the topic that commands the most attention in professional advice columns and blogs. Almost everyone finds it a stressful transition, even many of those who have every reason to believe that they are on the golden path to tenure.

The dichotomous nature of the tenure decision is part of the reason why it is so stressful. You don't slide easily into tenure; you go through a formal review that concludes in an up or out decision in most places. In a minority of institutions and for some disciplines, the process is divided into two discrete steps: first, promotion to associate professor and, later, tenure (job security), but typically these transitions are yoked together. In other fields such as law, getting tenure is accompanied by a move from assistant to full professor in a single step. However it occurs, tenure is the most important divide in academic life. And perhaps for that reason, the institution of tenure is imperiled. Many colleges and universities, especially those that are primarily devoted to teaching, are abandoning tenure in favor of a series of continuous reappointments. Currently less than a third of all academic positions are on a tenure track, and the proportion has been steadily declining over the past several decades. Thus, many readers will find this section irrelevant to their own circumstances and can skip it. If you are fortunate enough to be on a tenure track—although many might consider themselves fortunate not to face tenure—then read on.

The process of evaluation typically begins at the end of five years and takes place during the sixth year of the assistant professorship. (A growing number of places now allow leaves for maternity or paternity that can delay the decision by pausing the tenure clock.) Candidates can sometimes defer the tenure process until the final year of their contract, but this is hazardous because you may have to forgo the possibility of having a year after the tenure decision to look around for another job. The reality is that if you are on a tenure track, your appointment generally cannot extend beyond seven years as an assistant professor, which is a relatively short portion of an academic life.

Occasionally, people ask or are invited to apply for tenure earlier than in the sixth year either because their performance is outstanding or because they have an outside offer of tenure. This is more likely to occur in top-tier universities and in fields where there is aggressive recruitment for younger stars. If you go up early, be certain that you have the full backing of your department. Personnel reviews at higher levels will discourage early tenure unless the case is very solid and there is a real prospect of losing the candidate to another university. Never overstate your position or try to bluff your department into an early tenure decision unless you are willing and able to leave!

Normally, candidates prepare their dossiers for review and update their materials during their sixth year. As I mentioned earlier, the criteria for tenure vary enormously depending on discipline and department. Rarely do candidates receive an explicit statement of what is required to obtain tenure. Most evidence from faculty surveys suggests that by the time that they face tenure, most academics indicate that they understand the standards for being promoted in their department. The more ambiguous part of the process, one that sometimes ignites controversy and even lawsuits, is judging whether they have indeed met these standards.

The tenure assessment normally occurs at a number of levels of review: at a committee level in the department, in a vote by the full department of tenured faculty, at the administrative unit in which the department is embedded, and at the university level (the provost, president, and board of trustees). This series of steps or hoops that must be cleared is another reason that the process is so harrowing. If you are an anxious type or have a streak of paranoia, the tenure review is going to be difficult. Even if you don't, it is often an arduous process nonetheless because there are so many discrete steps along the way.

The first, and usually most important, step occurs by a unanimous or overwhelming endorsement of your department. How your case is assembled and presented to your colleagues matters, and you have the most influence in this part of the process. Well before you confront the process, you should look at successful applications for tenure in your institution to get a good sense of what is involved in putting together your dossier.

Along with your curriculum vita, you will be asked to prepare a statement about your research and often a separate statement about your approach toward and success in teaching. In institutions that strongly value service to the larger community, you may also have to write an account of your community activities. Remember that colleagues, reviewers, and administrators will read this statement, so you must prepare it with care and attention to detail. You should write it thematically to make a case that you have delivered the goods. If the statements you used for applying for the position and for reappointment were carefully drafted, they represent good starting points for your tenure statements. You can refer back to them to show how your research, teaching, and service contributions have evolved during your years in the department.

You should understand that only some of your colleagues have the skills and knowledge to understand or assess your research contributions. Teaching has a simple metric of evaluation: course evaluations and recommendations from former students. In some instances, colleagues may actually evaluate your performance in the classroom. Your service and collegial qualities are also fairly easy to appraise. But the fact is that most of us cannot judge our colleagues' scholarly contributions well unless we are in a similar or closely related field. This is well understood in the sciences, and in varying degrees in the social sciences and humanities. This is why letters from senior figures in your specialty field count for so much in the evaluation process, particularly in research-oriented colleges and universities. At the top tier, where outside letters play an inordinately important role in the tenure decision, a couple of bad letters can kill a candidate's prospects for tenure if not effectively countered by a chair's letter of recommendation.

Normally, the candidate has some input in selecting the referees. They are often able to nominate a list of possible reviewers, and some of their selections may be accepted by their department and endorsed by the university, but they will typically be a minority of the reviewers recruited by tenure committee members (or specialists in the department in the same field) and administrators in charge of tenure reviews. In my lifetime, the number of outside evaluators has grown from roughly six to ten or twelve, and occasionally more, imposing a huge burden on senior scholars who are asked to review tenure files in other departments.

If you are invited to submit candidates for review, pick wisely from your network of contacts. You want to select senior figures, usually full professors, who know of and appreciate your scholarly contributions. Standards vary as to whether you are permitted to select former thesis advisors, collaborators, and sponsors with whom you have worked. Generally speaking, it's best to take well-known scholars from your special area of expertise with whom you have not worked closely. They will have the most credibility, but you should not hesitate to draw from the people whose opinions you trust. Many departments also allow you to indicate potential reviewers with whom you may have taken issue in your previous research and therefore might be biased in evaluating your work. You have some control over the list, but you will often not even know some of the scholars who evaluate your file. This is yet another reason why the tenure process is stressful. Your scholarly work ultimately is subjected to a meta-evaluation from members of the academy with whom you may not even be acquainted.

Ultimately, the tenure system, especially as it is practiced in research universities and colleges, relies heavily on your professional reputation—how highly others in your field value your work and appreciate your contribution to date and potential in the future. The emphasis on professional reputation means that reviews from eminent figures in your field have great weight in the decision. In the top universities and places aspiring to move up in their national rankings, reviews are extensive, sometimes running to several pages from each reviewer. In many fields, reviewers are asked to compare or rank candidates against their recently tenured peers. Committees scrutinize these letters, parsing the language to interpret evaluations that are not completely explicit. Tenure deliberation can sometimes take on the quality of an exegesis of religious texts and not infrequently generate contention within a department. Increasingly, tenure reviews have introduced quantitative assessments that draw on citation counts or variants designed to measure professional influence. The problem in such approaches is that citations occur more slowly in some fields than in others, especially when books count more than articles.

Some disciplines, most typically in the humanities, regard books as essential for tenure; other fields deem them as irrelevant and only count articles, such as in the natural sciences and behavioral sciences. In my field of sociology, there are departments that lean one way or the other depending on their intellectual orientation. It is a peculiar feature of academia that what counts may vary across disciplines and departments. For example, among the top-ranked departments in economics, the only thing that counts is at least one publication in one of the leading journals in the field. Other contributions may be heavily discounted. In other fields, the quantity of work, measured by number of publications, may be most important to a candidate's success in the tenure process. It is critical that you have a clear sense of what counts in your department and in your field, because it will be reflected in the reviewers' letters.

In an ideal world, this review process would yield a clear and consistent outcome for a given candidate. And it frequently works that way at the extremes, when a case is very strong or very weak. However, tenure evaluations tend to follow a bell curve, so most cases fall in the middle of the distribution. This reality leaves a great deal of room for differences of opinion.

My graduate students often ask me how much of a role departmental politics plays in the tenure process. It is a hard question to answer because it depends on what counts as political. If we mean by "political" that senior colleagues in the department, or those higher up in the administrative process, try to influence the outcome to conform to their evaluation of the case, the answer is certainly yes. This happens more in cases where the decision is a close call. People hold different standards of how much a candidate should accomplish; members of a department value teaching contributions differently; and there is often no perfectly consistent evaluation in the letters for a given candidate. Moreover, the opinions of specialists in the same or closely related fields often are taken more seriously in the deliberations, as they usually should be, because these specialists are presumably more capable of judging the quality of the work.

However, there is little question that other factors, less germane to the candidate's record of accomplishment, can and often do enter into the tenure decision. Consider the much-publicized case of a scholar in a journalism department who was initially denied and subsequently granted tenure on appeal because even though he had a strong record of scholarly contribution, some of his colleagues thought he was difficult, even abusive in his dealings. Others swore by his integrity, even though he was regarded as abrupt and outspoken—qualities that are hardly unusual in academia.[9] Department politics figured in this case, even though the scholar in question had a strong academic record. Being well liked and personally well regarded also count in less conspicuous ways, although, to my knowledge, no one has measured the influence of personal relationships within departments in tenure decisions. Clearly, it helps to get along with your colleagues, particularly in your department. A strong consensus in the department on a tenure case is a good but imperfect predictor of ultimate success.

After the department vote, which typically happens in the autumn of the sixth year, the chair sends the case to the dean's office along with a cover letter. In smaller colleges and separate administrative units in a university, the department review could represent the penultimate decision; in larger universities, the case is usually referred to a personnel committee representing a number of different disciplines. In either case, the chair often has great latitude in framing the case for the next levels. He or she summarizes the department's assessments and makes the case for granting or denying tenure. The opinion of the chair, who has a role in the department as well as the administration, may have great weight, especially if he or she is well regarded by the administration and colleagues outside the department who may serve on the college or university personnel committee. Chairs will often take great care to represent the department's views, but they will not infrequently express their own opinions on the case. This is another point where considerations of political influence and resources can matter a lot. Strong departments tend to get their way; weak or less valued departments can lose out if the case is ambiguous, even if there is a strong departmental vote.

The second review, which generally is the purview of an interdisciplinary committee of faculty members, involves an independent assessment of the candidate's case and the departmental process. In some instances, this may be a rubber stamp, but more often the review is far from pro forma. Academics are paid to display and exercise critical sensibilities, and they usually do so when they serve on a personnel committee where they are invited to examine the standards that other disciplines exercise, which are frequently different from their own. Again, I have not located any statistics on how often departmental decisions are reversed in this second round of review, but it certainly happens not infrequently and undoubtedly in some institutions more than others. Well-presented cases from well-regarded departments may be rarely reversed, but the fate of weaker candidates can be uncertain, especially if the chair's letter is not powerful or the department's vote is split. By this point in the process, the tenure candidate can do little but watch and wait.

There is a third level of review after the university personnel committee has rendered its decision. The dean reviews the case and guides it through an administrative review, which may be another level of scrutiny. Some institutions require a completely independent review by outside faculty at this point. In any event, the administration has a right to reject or accept departmental and university personnel decisions. Sometimes these decisions rely heavily on earlier reviews, but when prior decisions have been difficult or controversial, academic administrators are likely to exercise a heavier hand.

Tenure is not officially granted until the board of trustees of a college or university ratifies the decision. Except for rare instances that invariably make the pages of the newspapers and trade journals, this level of approval is pro forma. Political interference by the trustees is regarded as infringement on academic freedom, and most universities do not want to be in a position of denying promotions to worthy candidates on political grounds. It damages the reputation of the institution.

It is a wonder that the process produces successful outcomes given the baroque complexity of decision making. It does, but I cannot provide any definitive statistics on the general rate of success in the tenure process. Longitudinal data following appointments over time are rare indeed, and there is no source of data on what proportion of tenure decisions are approved. One careful study of scientists in Research I universities (institutions with intensive research programs) shows that roughly half of all tenure cases are approved. This does not take full account of the fact that the weakest candidates have dropped out somewhere along the way either in reappointment or, as sometimes happens, prior to the tenure decision if they are advised that they will not make it. Men's chances are higher than women's in science and engineering disciplines.[10] Whether or not this rate of success could be generalized to other fields is anyone's guess. Recently Penn State compiled the rate of success for its faculty and also reported that half of applications for tenure were successful.[11]

In a not-negligible number of cases that have been turned down initially, the department or candidate successfully petitions for a re-review the following year. Additional scholarly work, fresh letters, or efforts to address weaknesses in the dossier by the chair can reverse the decision. Occasionally, a candidate will pursue a legal course of action if he or she believes that the process or decision has been manifestly unfair. This is an extreme remedy that you should pursue only if there is clear evidence of malfeasance in the tenure process. If you follow this course, be sure that you are not the only one who believes that you are in the right. It takes a toll on everyone, especially you, because it is invariably expensive and time-consuming, and it diverts most of your energy away from your work.

Being turned down for tenure is humiliating even if there are valid reasons, and most candidates do not feel that the outcome is valid or they wouldn't have sought a promotion. It can damage your reputation and make it difficult to find another job. However, it is rarely the end of the line for academics, and, surprisingly, in most instances rejected candidates go on to find another job, sometimes even at a comparable or better institution. I can count a large number of cases, including some of my own students and former colleagues, where assistant professors were turned down for tenure and went on to get good appointments elsewhere. Indeed, some places regard denial of tenure elsewhere as a recruiting opportunity. Being rejected for promotion is probably less stigmatizing than many would believe because everyone understands that the process of evaluation is imperfect and judgments often differ in the assessment of a candidate's work. I daresay that a lot of ranking departments have members who are refugees of the tenure process from another institution.

Being rejected for tenure is nonetheless a test of character and commitment. It requires a certain amount of self-confidence to pick up the pieces and move elsewhere. Rejected candidates sometimes speak of being treated like ghosts by their colleagues. At the same time, a lot of encouragement can be forthcoming from supporters in the department and your mentors and friends elsewhere. Being turned down for tenure is a painful event, but not infrequently it can turn out to be a blessing in disguise for the injured party because he or she ends up moving to a department that provides a better fit.

Because tenure decisions are frequently close calls, supportive senior faculty can be important allies in getting another job. Their testimony to your talents and accomplishments means a lot, so it is usually in your interest to accept the outcome and solicit advice and assistance from your colleagues in your efforts to make a transition to another department. People who handle the decision with dignity often find that colleagues, even those who were less than fully supportive, may begin to express seller's remorse.

One question that often comes up when tenure is denied is whether you must start the process all over again. The answer is usually no. Occasionally, people can move from a higher- to a lower-ranked institution that grants them tenure immediately. More often they must serve for from one to three years as an assistant (or in some places an associate without tenure) professor before they come up for review in their new institution. This provides ample time to build a stronger case for promotion. The people who are successful the second time around are often those who are determined to prove to their former colleagues and institutions that they made a mistake in letting them go. And they often do!

ON THE FAR SIDE OF TENURE

Let's assume that you are among the fortunate and have been granted tenure in your own department or because you successfully migrated to a position with tenure elsewhere. Most newly tenured faculty members are in their late thirties or early forties. By this point you have spent upward of fifteen years, and possibly more, in the academy as a graduate student, postdoc, adjunct, and assistant professor. You are no longer an apprentice or a journeyman; you are now a member of the guild. The stages leading up to tenure constitute roughly the first third of your academic career. Lest you think that you will be able to coast along in the next third, read on.

4

ACADEMIC MIDLIFE

Like the notion of midlife itself, the beginning of the middle third of academic life is inherently ambiguous because it does not start until promotion to tenure or its equivalent (attaining promotion and a measure of job security). Surprisingly, I could find no reliable national statistics for the age by which individuals on a tenure track are promoted to the position of associate professor. Recognizing that this transition may never occur for some readers, I estimate that most physical and natural scientists holding tenure-track jobs have attained tenure by their mid- to late thirties; social scientists generally reach this milestone a year or two later, and in the humanities, the tenure decision may come another year or two later.[1] Of course, a lot of academics who do not enter tenure-track positions right after graduate school may be still trying to find a greater measure of security even in their late forties. Promotion often occurs much earlier in the higher tier of universities and colleges. Yet by their mid-forties, most PhDs who are seeking an academic career have found a teaching job or a stable administrative post that more or less suits their needs. The great majority of readers by this point in their lives will feel as though they have settled into an academic career, albeit one with varying degrees of job security and contentment.

It may seem odd to many readers to devote three chapters to the beginning of an academic career, one to the middle years that span another third to a half of an academic's life, and the last chapter to the final stage of an academic career. I suppose this reflects a somewhat misleading notion that nothing of great importance really happens in midlife![2] Of course, this idea is completely inaccurate, but it certainly reflects the general discussion of academic life in the trade journals and even in the scholarly literature. As I noted in earlier chapters, there are lengthy discussions about managing graduate school and its immediate aftermath as well as a huge literature on being an assistant professor and especially the tenure process. But my collection of articles and clippings drops off dramatically when it comes to the rest of an academic's life. The final two-thirds command—by my rough estimate—less than a quarter of all the attention received in the advice columns and firsthand accounts of being an academic.

It is true that getting there is a lot more stressful than being there. Much more learning and seasoning is required in the first third of an academic career than in the years that follow. Still, senior academics have plenty to say about problematic features of managing life in universities and colleges. This chapter will address some of these issues.

A few years back, I gave a luncheon seminar devoted to mentoring young scholars at the Population Association of America, the professional organization for demographers, sociologists, and behavioral scientists who do work on issues related to population. Afterward, the organizer of the seminar, a successful associate professor at a leading university who had sat in on my talk, remarked to me: "Someone ought to give a similar seminar for people at my stage in academic life. No one ever prepared me for what happens after I was promoted." I spent the next hour listening to her concerns: managing a growing workload, taking on too many administrative tasks, difficulty in finding the next big project, and so on. The almost exclusive focus on young academics certainly misses a large number of characteristic dilemmas that come after settling into academic life. To list but a few of the ones that I will discuss in this chapter are such challenges as assuming the responsibilities of running and maintaining a well-functioning department, finding time for scholarship, achieving work/family balance, and, of course, making the transition from associate to full professor. True, the Sturm und Drang has abated, but there are important, even critical, issues and events after reaching professional maturity that must be successfully navigated in order to maintain a high level of contentment in the middle years of an academic career.

For most academics who went through the tenure process or worked their way into a stable and secure non-tenure-track position, the transition in retrospect feels like a challenging ski jump. You managed to land on your feet and feel a sense of exhilarating accomplishment for having done so; for a small number, the road to tenure may feel more like a near-death experience. In either case, you now face a different sort of adjustment when you are no longer "junior" faculty; suddenly you are called upon to start pulling your weight in your department and, often, your discipline or home academic institution. For the first time in your life, you can begin to look ahead with a sense of confidence that you are likely to be around for a while in your chosen profession. At the same time, moving up the ladder creates a new set of dilemmas and challenges.

I have been amazed at the range of reactions to the post-tenure experience that I have witnessed among my colleagues and former students over the years. Most simply breathe a sigh of relief and dig into their work, beginning to enjoy a new sense of independence. As one of my younger colleagues wrote me after reading an earlier draft of this chapter, the greatest reward of tenure is "the ability to pursue topics that might be risky otherwise." He went on to say that midlife provided him with an opportunity to consolidate his research agenda and "to expand a bit on the perimeter." A small minority is not unscathed by the transition after having been scrutinized and evaluated for such a lengthy duration during their years of apprenticeship. I will get to them in a moment, but I want to reiterate that the vast majority I've witnessed during the transition is simply glad it is behind them. They understand and appreciate that they have entered a new stage of academic life, one that permits and even demands a package of new responsibilities.

Suddenly, your department chair expects you to take on a greater role in administering the department, graduate students begin to flock to you for advice and support, and your collaborators are insisting that now it is your turn to write the proposal to renew your grant. It is a nice change, but the new demands may hit you too abruptly. You had expected to have a bit more time to spend with the family, to investigate a new research area, or to pursue leisure activities in the evenings or on weekends, but much to your surprise you find yourself, if anything, working harder than ever. "Wait," you may be saying, "I don't want to work this hard after tenure." Or your family may be saying to you, "I thought you said that after you got tenure you would have more time for us." I am afraid I must tell you that life after tenure does not usually result in a lot more free time for academics—at least, not in the beginning of the post-tenure years. Most of you will discover that your situation is a lot less stressful on the whole, but new demands appear to replace the old ones. As one academic recalls, "I was being asked (told?) to accept new responsibilities and assignments beyond my comfort level and outside the close confines of my disciplinary expertise. I felt both exulted (at being asked) and pressured (at being 'told')."[3]

That is bad enough, but for a few of you—I won't even hazard a guess of the actual number because of a complete absence of statistical data on the topic—the post-tenure experience ushers in a new crisis of confidence rather than settling your doubts about what you are doing with your life. There are many reasons why this happens. For those of you who are close calls in the tenure process, you may be simply worn out by the ups and downs of a long year or two. A friend of mine at a top university barely survived a bruising tenure battle many years ago; he never quite recovered from the experience and has had trouble writing ever since. Still an associate professor twenty years later after his tenure battle, he continues to brood about how his life would have been different were it not for the ugly fight that he had to endure.

Some new associate professors talk in dramatic terms, saying they have "survivors' guilt." Having seen friends and peers flounder in the process, they cannot easily accept their own success. Others get over the hump, only to find themselves plagued by doubts about whether they have the stamina to spend a lifetime doing what they had to do over the past ten or so years.[4] Occasionally, newly appointed associate professors find that once they have succeeded in gaining tenure, they lose interest in the academic game altogether and want a different sort of challenge. It is strange, but some of us get up for challenges but feel down when they are over. After showing that they could make it through the long, arduous tenure process, some now begin to question whether they want to continue to work in academia or would prefer to do something else. It is not so unusual for younger academics—even, or perhaps especially, when they have been successful—to begin to ask themselves tough questions about their commitment to the profession once they have surmounted the tenure challenge.

If you find yourself slightly depressed and disillusioned after the tenure process, I can assure you that your feelings, though fairly uncommon, are far from exceptional. Most people do not like the feeling of being judged by their colleagues, even if the judgments end up being positive. Perhaps you heard something about the details of the decision-making process: you may find yourself wondering just which two senior colleagues in your department voted against your promotion. The uncertainty that occurs in the promotion process can generate anger and even paranoia. Like troubled courtships that end in success, the feelings of uncertainty sometimes linger even after the situation is resolved.

I will devote some attention in this chapter to ways of renewing commitment, managing enhanced responsibilities, and finding or making time for you and your family, among other things, but a few words are warranted for the relatively rare cases of people who find themselves at a loss after the tenure decision. If these feelings persist beyond a few months, you should consider seeking help in working through the negative responses that you cannot let go of. Don't allow yourself to get stuck in post-tenure limbo, where time goes by and you find yourself unable to work, as my friend did.

If you find yourself with little or no appetite for work—or the opposite, compelled to work constantly—and these sentiments linger, you should recognize both this opportunity and the necessity of renewing and reinvigorating your professional fantasies or ridding yourself of the feeling that you must be working compulsively or else. Take seriously the fact that you are telling yourself something—you don't like what you've been doing, or you don't like how you've been doing it. This is one of those times that you need to figure out a better way of engaging as an academic, or otherwise you could lose a sense of direction in the years ahead.

The vast majority of you, I hasten to add, will find that you feel more rather than less energy and enthusiasm for your work in the post-tenure years. In fact, this is a happy time in the lives of most academics, especially those who have found a department where they like most of their colleagues, have become reasonably comfortable managing their teaching load, and have gotten into the habit of research and writing. Indeed, a lot of associate professors will discover that their appetites for taking on new challenges exceed their capacities or at least the time they have to fulfill all their tasks. As far as I am concerned, this is the major challenge in academic midlife—how to do all the things you want to do and to continue doing them reasonably well. There may be a tendency at this point in your career to feel as though you can and should say yes to all of the attractive possibilities that come along while also feeling an obligation to accept some of the less attractive demands on your time.

The big question for you is learning to take on more but not more than you can possibly do in a reasonable working week. I can vividly recall a time, shortly after I got tenure, when I found myself in a horrible situation: I had promised to write eight papers over the next three months. How foolish could I have been to have said yes to so many requests? I was in a state of panic and found myself working far more than the fifty to fifty-five hours per week that I considered a reasonable commitment to my job. I don't quite know how I did it, but somehow I managed to get through that awful period, and I resolved to never allow myself to get into that situation again. I have kept that resolution more or less throughout the rest of my career. It is absolutely imperative that you learn to say no even to attractive possibilities. More about how to regulate the work flow later on, but the first rule of successful survival in academic midlife is to maintain a reasonable work schedule by avoiding taking on more than you can handle. I must admit that it is one of those rules that are easier to say than to practice.

Figure out how much you are willing to work, understanding, of course, that there will be some occasional busy periods that require more time than you have bargained for. Academics have different tastes for working and different constraints and commitments, aside from the need for leisure time, that interfere with work life. My preference, as I said earlier, was to keep my work schedule to no more than fifty to fifty-five hours per week. I have always had colleagues who work more and, no doubt, some who work less. But don't let yourself get into a macho match to see if you work the most among your peers, unless you really like playing that sort of game.

It is also important to learn to be realistic about how long things actually take you—almost always longer than you imagine. Work routines, which I discussed in earlier chapters, help a lot. It is hard to budget your time when you don't have a schedule. The people I know who manage their workload best are those who operate more or less on a regular schedule because they know when to start and when to stop. Unless dire emergencies arise, they more or less keep to their work schedules and routines. It is not easy to do, but creating a reasonable work schedule goes a long way toward keeping you sane. Remember what I said in the first chapter: the nature of a successful academic career means that you are almost always in debt—you owe something to someone. So, an essential rule of survival is managing your debt load.

Happily, most people find that virtually all of the things you found to be difficult at the onset of your career get easier over time. Teaching requires a lot of up-front time in the early years, but most of us realize that with experience our courses require a lower time commitment unless you take on a new course preparation. By this point, you are likely to be comfortable in the lecture hall or seminar room. You can work on perfecting your techniques of communication, introduce new materials, and figure out novel ways of engaging students in assignments, and these efforts should only call for minor adjustments. In the next chapter, I will cover the problem that some of us face when teaching becomes boring and unrewarding —something that usually does not happen to faculty in the early post-tenure years.

Research and writing tend to become easier too. By now, you have accumulated a good deal of experience in crafting research regardless of your field of study. You probably would not have gotten to where you are if you hadn't demonstrated an ability to conduct research on interesting problems. As my colleague described earlier, your ambitions will probably grow during the middle years of your career, since you have more time to invest in longer and larger projects. My single bit of advice here is simple: Try to shape your agenda so that you have a combination of short-term and long-term projects, because your colleagues are looking for a steady pattern of productivity. You may care more about the next big project before you have even finished the last one, but it is desirable to manage a portfolio of research that pays steady dividends in the form of good publications. This means finishing some of the pesky projects that lie on your desk and need a few days or weeks of attention before you can get them back to a journal that has asked for revisions.

Most academics—especially in the social sciences and humanities, where crafting a professional paper involves a seemingly endless process of revisions—do not especially enjoy cleaning up their papers, responding to criticisms of colleagues and reviewers, and getting the paper out the door. It is much more fun to go on to the next thing, thinking that you will get back to the additions that must be made before sending a paper off for review or re-review. The result is that papers can pile up and run the risk of being dated by the work of others in your field. While we academics hate deadlines, they are probably our salvation for getting work completed.

SERVING YOUR DEPARTMENT AND UNIVERSITY

I already alluded to the tricky problem of academic midlife: the increased demand for service to your department, your college or university, your discipline, or perhaps to the surrounding community.[5] Departmental life is organized through committees, and you will suddenly find that you are being asked to chair this activity or that program. Whereas you have some grounds for being protected when you are still a junior faculty member, this shield, if it was ever provided, disappears after promotion to seniority. If anything, your fellow senior colleagues are likely to believe that you "owe them" after you become tenured for the protection that they provided earlier on. There is nowhere to hide and no way to avoid taking on a greater measure of responsibility in academic affairs and administration. Some academics relish the chance to participate in the management of their departments, while others try to avoid committee work as much as possible. Those who make themselves scarce when it comes to administration tasks can sometimes get away with doing less, but they are understandably resented by their colleagues who must shoulder a larger load of the housework. Colleagues who do more for their departments are often rewarded by being asked to do still more, especially if they perform their administrative duties competently. This is where careers begin to diverge.

What is the right amount of service for you to being doing at mid-career? In the last chapter, I suggested that service activities of all types should not require much more than a day per week of your time when you are an assistant professor, depending, of course, on the type of academic institution. (Research-intensive institutions generally require lower commitments of service.) I'm afraid that many of you probably won't get away with that little amount of time after you enter mid-career. But you do have to set some limits unless your time is freed from teaching responsibilities. Otherwise, you must assume that the time required for service will eat into your research and writing and teaching preparation. By now, you know all too well that very few academic institutions give you much credit for departmental service. When you are "invited" to take on a service assignment, you can sometimes bargain with your chair or the administration for some kind of compensation in the form of money or released time, often in the future. If the assignment that you are asked to do is arduous, you can try to ask for a course release or a sabbatical in return. Sometimes you may even get it! But you are more likely to find out that it is simply part of your job description.

There is mounting evidence showing that women are more likely to say yes to requests for service than men, or at least that women seem to end up assuming a disproportionate share of the service workload. Beware of the consequences of being unduly generous when it comes to service. Even if you don't resent it at the time, you might later on if your promotion to full professor is delayed because you have had too little time to publish. Women on average spend several more years at the associate professor level.[6] Some of this time may accrue because of family responsibilities (another area where men are generally able to get away with doing less). If women end up doing more supervising of students, teaching an extra course here or there, and doing more service, these inequities will take a toll on the quality of department life.[7]

One of my friends remarked that she only began to detect a pattern of sexism in her department *after* she was promoted.

Departments where members willingly—albeit usually with a certain amount of good-natured griping—pitch in to carry the load of committee work benefit as a collectivity. Typically, colleagues are more appreciative and respectful of one another in these departments. There is a great benefit to those departments where civility and collegiality reigns. People show up at colloquia, they actively recruit new members, and they are able to join together when necessary. There is a sense of goodwill, and members can draw upon it when necessary. Most surveys of academic departments indicate that the majority of faculty have favorable views of their departments, suggesting that the stereotype of fractious relationships may be somewhat exaggerated.[8] I can tell you from personal experience that departmental infighting can consume an enormous amount of time with very little to show for the hours spent.

ACADEMIC WORK

The composition of academic work varies enormously by ranking and type of institution. At the top of the prestige ladder, where the teaching load is generally lighter, expectations for getting research grants and publishing are inevitably higher; at lower-tier institutions, the demands for teaching and community service may be greater, even though expectations for research and professional participation can still remain high. It is nearly impossible to do everything that you are asked to do and do it well. As in earlier stages of your career, you must do some strategizing about how to balance your priorities with the institution where you are employed. In other words, you must take careful account of whether the institutional expectations and your personal goals are aligned. Ask yourself if there are any colleagues in your department whom you want to emulate in the way that they manage their work life. If there are none, maybe you should be asking why not. Are you being unrealistic in your goals, or are you simply at the wrong institution to make a good fit for your particular ambitions? I'll come to what to do if the answer to that question is yes.

There is, of course, some differentiation of the tastes and talents of departmental members. Some people gravitate to doing more service because they are good at it, think that they can do a better job than most of their colleagues, like running things, or are simply more generous with their time. These people are often respected, and frequently their efforts are appreciated; however, they may also be exploited by their less willing and able colleagues. If you gravitate toward a leadership role in departmental administration, make sure that you are doing so willingly. I sometimes hear from friends or former students that they are not getting enough time to do teaching and research—the things that attracted them to academia. You don't want to find yourself in that position for more than a limited period of time. If it becomes a chronic situation, you need to assert yourself or redefine your goals. It is bound to be the case that some readers will find that their predilection for research diminishes after tenure, and they actually begin to prefer the administrative tasks of running a department or serving their institution. That is almost a sure sign that you may be headed into administration in years to come. There is nothing wrong with that, so long as you see it as a choice rather than something that is being imposed upon you against your wishes. I have little sympathy for victims of administrative responsibilities who claim that their careers were diverted because they felt unable to turn down an administrative request in their institution.

Just recently, I had lunch with a former colleague of mine who had a relatively easy time of gaining tenure in a school of public policy. But in the past eight years, he had worked hard in developing a new curriculum for his school as part of a national reform in his specialty. It took countless hours, and though the administrative planning had been rewarding, his scholarly production had lagged and his professional reputation had suffered. Now in his early fifties, he faced a dilemma: should he continue to be an administrator at the expense of his academic work, or should he return to doing research in hopes of gaining a promotion to full professor? Not an easy choice. After a lengthy discussion, we settled on a strategy that involved telling his colleagues that he must now largely withdraw from his administrative responsibilities for the next three or four years to commit himself to a program of research to test the effects of the curriculum reforms that he and his colleagues had developed. Whether he is successful or not, he thought that he would feel better returning to research before it was too late.

MANAGING MULTIPLE PROFESSIONAL ACTIVITIES

No matter how well you manage it, the demands for professional service in your discipline will probably rise as you move into the midlife of your career. In the normal course of things, you will get more invitations to serve your disciplinary organizations, give talks in other departments, participate in research projects, and author chapters and papers. As you advance in your career, most will find themselves moving into a different "opportunity structure," as we sociologists characterize it. Specifically, as you become better known, acquire more social contacts, and your professional world is expanded, invitations and entreaties often begin to exceed your capacity, if only because professional activity tends to beget more professional activity. My colleague Annette Laureau contends that paradoxically being *outside* the limelight offers some advantages to younger scholars against the onslaught of professional requests that can distract them from scholarly accomplishment in the early years of an academic career.[9]

But, if you are like most younger academics, you will find that these requests are attractive if not downright enticing. I know that I did. It is flattering to be asked to run for a professional office, at least the first time it happens. Likewise, it is difficult to turn down the opportunity to write a chapter for a special issue of a journal devoted to a topic of interest or a new area of research that you are thinking of entering. A senior colleague at a distinguished university is holding a small research conference, and you are asked to participate. How can you possibly say no? A close friend whom you have known since your graduate student days wants you to give a colloquium in her department. You are eager to catch up with her and use the opportunity to get to know some of her colleagues. You get the picture: suddenly, you find yourself inundated with a flood of new professional opportunities and feel helpless to resist them.

There is no denying it: being in demand feels heady. What doesn't necessarily feel so good is figuring out how to get all of these things done once you've agreed to them. Humans are not very good at projecting themselves into the future. Discounting future time commitments is a familiar scholarly topic in economics and psychology. And academics are no better than anyone else at imagining the amount of time it takes to complete the work they take on. Before you know it, you are completely snowed under by obligations that you agreed to six months or a year ago when you thought you would have plenty of time to get it all done. Pretty soon you end up like I did, having agreed to write eight papers in the next three months. Well, there is very little to be done once you are in this situation.

Not that we academics never renege on our commitments, but it is considered really bad form to back out of a talk or a paper that you've promised for a conference. There is no particular punishment except the scorn of your colleagues, but for most of us, that is a pretty severe sanction. If you get the reputation for being unreliable (and most unreliable professors never realize this even after they acquire it), you will make a lot of people unhappy with you. Unless you have very tough skin, it doesn't feel good to let your professional colleagues down. I have a friend who once declared that once in a lifetime every academic ought to be able to declare themselves bankrupted, but short of a severe illness or worse, there is no way of doing so without considerable cost to your reputation.

Here are some things that you can do to keep your professional accounts in balance. First, start budgeting your time for future work obligations. I know it is like counting calories, and it won't work for everyone, but give it a try. Allot a generous amount of time for the tasks that you are undertaking and see whether it all adds up to a reasonable schedule. If new requests come your way, see what you are able to defer (if anything) if you elect to take them on. This means having at least some general notion of how long it will take you to write a conference paper, including factoring in travel time. It may be difficult to do, but budgeting your time provides a metric for deciding whether you can "afford" to say yes to an invitation or, at least, what you may have to put off in order to have the time to take on a new task. Roughly, how many hours in a week or month must you allot for the commitments you make for teaching, service, and research and writing?

When you do take on added assignments of any type, it is helpful to consider where the time will come from. Can you give something up, or will you complete a task before the new obligation kicks in? Some readers may prefer to write all of this down and create a schedule for major professional activities. Whether you do this or not, the essential point is to avoid the assumption that somehow you will find the additional time in the face of your existing workload. There is a cruel paradox that must be confronted if your professional requests and invitations are expanding. You may think that you are getting better at saying no because you are turning down more requests. The real problem, though, is in the numerator—the absolute number of times you say yes—not the denominator of the total number of requests. If the denominator is growing rapidly, you can find yourself saying no more often but still taking on more than you can realistically manage.

Know when to stop. I said in an earlier chapter that perfectionism can be the enemy of productivity. You can spend an awful lot of time dithering on issues of no particular significance unless you take care to stop yourself. Try to have a proportional sense of the value and necessity of different parts of the work process. By mid-career, you should have a reasonable sense of when, whether, and how to cut certain corners and which corners simply cannot be cut at all.

I have sometimes advised desperately overworked colleagues to develop a decision matrix for determining whether to say yes or no to new requests. My stepdaughter, a molecular biologist, independently came upon this idea and showed me her matrix. It included a substantial list of considerations that she used in deciding to accept an invitation: Would it advance her research agenda, would it expose her to new colleagues and information, would it be fun (a not trivial consideration!), how much travel was involved (she has young kids and a spouse with high travel demands), and so on. She always waits for a day or two to think through the potential costs of accepting an invitation. The formality of making decisions in this way may strike some readers as mechanical and soulless, but it is likely to make you far more resistant to an automatic yes to whatever comes along. It may help to avoid the common complaint often heard uttered by overly busy academics: "Why in the world did I ever agree to do this?" The answer is that you were asked fourteen months ago, and it never occurred to you then that you would have better or more urgent things to do with your time now. Unless you exercise restraint in taking on future obligations, I can assure you that you will be bemoaning your decisions and wishing you had made better choices, because there is a high likelihood that you will be taking away more time than you want from your family or other priorities in your life. Refusing invitations does not come easily to most of us because we relish interest in our ideas and research. We like being asked, even sometimes when we wish that we had not been asked. I have always had a difficult time refusing requests. Yet it helps me to remember that I cannot think of a single invitation I have turned down that I later came to regret.

TEACHING AND RELATIONS WITH STUDENTS

Sometimes when I am visiting another university, I have an opportunity to wander the halls and observe: How many faculty members come in on any given day? How many doors are open along a corridor of offices? The signup sheets for appointments sometimes more than fill the available slots, and one gets the sense that students face severe problems in getting their faculty advisors to answer their pressing questions, much less be available for a more casual chat. In the earlier chapters, I viewed the communal life of the department as a problem primarily for students or young faculty members. As I remarked in previous chapters, departments in which students and faculty have only formal relations in the classroom or during office hours are not especially interesting places to work. When students and faculty have frequent and informal contact, they are typically more stimulating and lively places to be: the department feels more like a cohesive neighborhood than a corporate headquarters.

Students are a tremendous source of professional pleasure and pride. They also require a lot of tending and hand holding. If you like mentoring, as I do, then you must budget ample time to care for your students. Otherwise, they will become a residual category, orphaned by your other obligations. In many research universities and even in institutions that are primarily devoted to teaching, there are professors who really prefer to confine their contacts with students to the classroom and designated office hours. More often, I have witnessed faculty who like mentoring students but really do not allocate enough time to do it.

Of course, institutional expectations partly influence the climate that evolves in departments. As an undergraduate, I went to Haverford College and was spoiled when it came to faculty contact. Students had the expectation that you could (and maybe even should) feel free to drop in the office of a faculty member at your convenience. It was not unusual even to drop by on a weekend to say hello to a faculty member at their home. I experienced a culture shock when I entered Columbia as a graduate student, where it was then considered inappropriate to visit a faculty member without a prior appointment. Graduate students generally felt that they had to have a good, if not compelling, reason to call upon faculty members. Some of my colleagues at research-intensive universities would say that this is how it should be.

Faculty members have very different sensibilities about their obligations to students. Some are exceedingly generous with their time; others provide help sparingly, grudgingly, or not at all. However, most of us are in the business of teaching to educate, if not to shape, the minds of young people. If you resent the demands on your time made by undergraduates, much less graduate students if you are in a research institution, you are probably in the wrong business. That is not to say, if you are in a research university, that undergraduate teaching should or will consume as much time as it requires in an institution that primarily caters to undergraduates. Most undergraduate institutions hire and promote faculty who are both able teachers and are prepared to devote themselves to their students. The reward system generally reinforces the expectation that a large portion of your professional time will be devoted to your role as a teacher.

If you are at a research university that puts a high premium on graduate education, teaching responsibilities must be balanced between undergraduate education and graduate teaching. Relatively few faculty members in research-intensive institutions, in my experience, prefer teaching undergraduate to graduate courses. The simple reason is that it is more work and, if class sizes are large, often less rewarding. Graduate classes are smaller, more intimate, and often related to the ongoing research of the faculty. In recent years many top-tier universities have rightly, in my view, tried to get tenured professors to be more involved in undergraduate teaching. Symbolically, the importance of under-graduate teaching has been rewarded by awards, financial assistance for hiring undergraduates to work on research, and budgets for tak-ing students out to lunch. Tenure decisions now always include teach-ing evaluations, and poor or indifferent teachers are penalized in the tenure process. This is a welcome change from the bad old days when popular teachers were almost suspect in top universities.

When I arrived at Penn, the teaching of undergraduates was rel-egated to graduate students, assistant professors, and a token number of tenured faculty members who either preferred to teach undergradu-ates or were not actively engaged in research. Worse yet, the practice of subcontracting out teaching to adjunct faculty members was wide-spread. I remember once stopping outside of the classroom of an en-gaging minister and a sociologist by training who had been hired to teach the introductory course in our department. I watched for a while the rapt audience of students listening to his lecture. He was indeed entertaining, but there was almost no content to his lecture. I am happy to say that my university no longer countenances the practice of letting adjuncts do the bulk of undergraduate teaching, but, if anything, the practice has become more common in less well-endowed universities and colleges.

I should add that there is good intellectual justification for the role of adjunct faculty in teaching. Many adjuncts are actively engaged in research but may hold administrative posts that are full-time jobs. Teaching is a privilege, and many part-time faculty relish teaching. Other adjunct faculty may come from outside the university and are invited to teach because they can provide special training or access to later employment opportunities.[10] So, for example, in my department at Penn, we used to invite a distinguished jurist to teach a course as well as an activist lawyer. Students rated their experiences in these classes very highly and often found their courses stimulating as well as useful in helping them to form career paths after graduation.

At the least selective schools, a great deal of the undergraduate teaching is farmed out to part-timers who may be gifted instructors (or not) but are often overwhelmed by trying to piece together enough courses to earn an adequate living. These adjuncts are often living hand to mouth as they try to work their way into a more permanent position. Tenured faculty provide administrative backup and may be permitted to teach the more advanced courses in smaller classes. It is a difficult and often unhappy situation for both the permanent faculty and the adjuncts, who are able to enjoy few of the perks of academic life.[11]

TEACHING AT THE GRADUATE LEVEL

In the first chapter of this book, I observed that departments, even of similar rank and quality, care differently about the quality of graduate education. Departmental members, too, are remarkably varied in their preferences for training graduate students and supervising their doctoral research. I have witnessed faculty who really don't want to give graduate students the time of day and those to whom graduate students flock because they are willing to provide seemingly unlimited time and attention. Some faculty members seem to do double and triple duty, serving on exam committees and supervising dissertations, while others try to avoid these tasks as much as they can.

In the next chapter, I'll speak more about the essential role of "generativity" in the academy, the term coined by the noted psychologist Erik Erikson to describe how the process of human development poses new challenges and requirements as one moves into the later stages of the life course. Erikson argued that generativity becomes a more prominent feature in successful aging.[12] For all but the greatest scholars, our contribution to our students' development will probably be the greatest intellectual legacy of our academic careers. I have never seen any research explaining the development of generativity in an academic career. It probably shows up as early as graduate school, and as opportunities for teaching and mentoring expand, the demand and proclivity for investing in students continue to develop. In the next chapter, I will argue that its absence sometimes makes the conclusion of an academic career unrewarding, if not traumatic.

In many fields, collaboration with students is an essential part of graduate education and, increasingly, an important ingredient in teaching advanced undergraduates. It is almost impossible to learn how to do research and writing from a textbook or even from a course. It requires a lot of practice, monitoring, and feedback to develop these professional skills. That is the fun of teaching and supervising graduate students, but it takes lots of time to do it right. In the previous chapter, I recommended limiting the number of graduate students that you work with closely or, at least, whose dissertation committee you serve on. This becomes harder to do when you move into midlife. There are some tricks to handling a larger load of graduate students that I can share from personal experience.

First, try to align your teaching and supervision of graduate students. If you are permitted, and you usually are by mid-career, teach a research workshop that draws together students who may share your intellectual interests. My most pleasurable experiences in teaching graduate students have occurred in workshops of this type where it is possible to teach disciplinary issues of importance and how they can be translated into research projects. Naturally, different disciplines provide varied sorts of professional training, but finding students who pick up on the problems that interest you provides a big emotional kick. Let's face it, when one of your students gets excited about an idea in your area of expertise, it feels gratifying. You reexperience your own sense of excitement in ideas. Naturally, you must be careful not to encourage your students to replicate your work—tempting as that might be. However, when they are able to combine ideas that you have introduced to them with the ideas of others to produce their own unique contributions, it is very satisfying to witness. I never tired of seeing this process of regeneration occur.

Two direct by-products of graduate teaching occur, and each raises some professional issues that are differently managed across the disciplines. The first is that collaborations with students often sprout from graduate workshops and discussions between faculty and students. The second is that students begin to develop ideas of their own that may eventuate in a paper or dissertation. This process is both inevitable and often gratifying to students and faculty alike. But the intermingling of faculty and student ideas—the point of graduate education—can sometimes create problems in the training process.

Whether in the natural sciences, the social and behavioral sciences, or the humanities, there is a general consensus that ideas occur in particular social contexts where they are fed by discussion and interpersonal exchange. In this particular sense, ideas are socially produced.

The social nature of ideas can be the source of common pride or bitter dissension in the reckoning of authorship and credit as these ideas are translated into research projects and publications. The process itself is governed differently across fields in ways that can be confounding to students and often to faculty as well. For the most part, there are no clear-cut standards of "ownership." In the sciences, ideas and techniques can be patented, but intellectual ownership of many ideas in most academic fields is inherently ambiguous.

In physical and biological sciences (and there is certainly variation among disciplines), it is probably fair to say that authorship of products is partly preassigned: that is, if you work in a research lab, the faculty member who supports and typically supervises your research is usually considered to be part "owner" of ideas that develop in the lab. Often this is signified by joint authorship of publications with the lab director as the last author and, presumably, the person to whom a major source of credit is assigned. The junior collaborator may be the first author, if he or she produces much of the work, and, in the course of things, his or her work will be given a high amount of credit as well. Credit will ultimately be adjudicated by how the authorship is interpreted by various players—the authors, the reviewers, and colleagues who read and acknowledge the work.

In the humanities, collaboration and coauthorship occurs much less frequently. Tenured faculty are less likely to hand off their ideas unless they have decided in advance that they will not pursue them in research or if the project they propose is tangential to their interests. In other words, sharing ideas certainly occurs, but sharing authorship is less common. Of course, it happens not infrequently, but the process is uncharted. A young historian whom I know began to develop a project with one of his colleagues only to find that the senior person thought it was such a good idea for a paper that he planned to do it himself. I advised the young historian to let the project go because his senior colleague clearly was going to take advantage of him. The rules for collaboration are poorly articulated, and often senior figures will want to claim more credit than is deemed appropriate by juniors. This could be changing, as there is some movement in the humanities and history, in particular, to encourage more teamwork and collaboration.

In social sciences, collaboration happens all the time with no clear guidelines for how to adjudicate credit. When I was in graduate school, I approached a faculty member with a paper that I had written in a course taught by one of his colleagues, asking for advice about where it might be published. He made some editorial changes in the first couple of pages and suggested that he edit the rest and that we could coauthor the paper together. With some difficulty, I managed to turn down his invitation. Now, in fact, I am certain that this person saw that I was using and referencing his work in the paper and perhaps felt he deserved to be a coauthor, even if he had not participated in the process of research and writing. How to draw the lines of collaboration is never an easy matter in the social sciences.

It is a great boon to work with students. Finding the extra hands (and minds) means that, especially in midlife and beyond, it is highly advantageous to collaborate with "junior" partners. Here is the rub. Unlike the sciences, where certainly issues of authorship and credit arise but where preestablished conventions for coauthorship exist, collaboration in the social sciences is fraught with ambiguity. It is a potentially perilous part of graduate training, and I cannot articulate a professional policy that would be universally accepted. But I suggest that first and foremost, as you enter into collaborations that may flow from teaching or merely discussions, that by the time any project or paper is proposed, the rules of the collaboration have been discussed or, in some cases, even put in written form to reduce the element of uncertainty.

I know that this feels unseemly—almost like a prenuptial agreement—but it will save a lot of grief and prevent misunderstandings and resentments from occurring later on. There are different elements that figure into a collaboration: who develops the idea and proposes the collaboration, which person does the lion's share of the work in data collection or scholarly research and analysis, and who writes up the findings, to mention the most prominent features. Clearly, if a researcher approaches a graduate student, offers to hire her for a summer project, and the student produces data analysis and perhaps some research memos, her role is a junior one. Depending on how much work she does and what it consists of, she may only be acknowledged in a publication and not be granted the status of coauthor. But suppose the student approaches the faculty member and asks for advice on a project that she has in mind. It just so happens that the faculty member has data appropriate to the project and offers it to her with the understanding that he will consult in the analysis and writing of the project. In this instance, I think the shoe is clearly on the other foot. It behooves the faculty member to be generous, even if he or she ends up doing half the work and must use a heavy hand in rewriting a draft of the paper for publication. In this instance my advice would be don't collaborate unless you are prepared to give the student a break in the assignment of credit.

Collaborations often evolve, so it is difficult to say just who did exactly how much of what activity. Simple ideas are elaborated over time, new data are blended into the analysis, and so on. If you think the rules no longer apply, as the faculty member, you have the responsibility of speaking up and doing it sooner than later. If it is a close call, the benefits always ought to be slanted, in my view, toward the more vulnerable party—that is, the junior person. Tenure or seniority should never be an excuse for getting more of the credit; it is far better if the system works the other way. Capitalists almost always value their contribution more than the folks who are providing the sweat equity!

This is easier to do when you are an established full professor rather than an associate professor who is still trying to build a record. Here is an instance in which personality probably trumps position. Generosity does not come easily to some people (dare I say, especially to men more so than women). But my point is not to preach the virtues of generosity, but to alert readers to their own built-in biases that may lead them astray when it comes to sharing professional credit. If you are generative—training able students to think and write—you are fulfilling your role and positioning yourself for a happy final stage in your career. If you are professionally greedy, the credit you receive from your colleagues and especially your students may be more tarnished than you can ever imagine. Academics are paid off in part by their professional standing, but many are completely tone-deaf to recognizing that their reputation suffers permanently when they are known to be self-serving with students.

Handing off some of your good ideas to dissertation students always seems like a very sound investment to me. Most of your students will give you credit for the rest of your life for *their* success. In an individualistic society such as ours, where personal rather than collective production is highly rewarded, contributions to your students may not show up on your vita, but trust me: you will get a lot of credit from them and the students they go on to teach. For this reason alone, it is a wise investment and a source of tremendous and enduring gratification over time.

My point is that you can do well for your students and for yourself at the same time by dissertation supervision and collaboration. If you are generous, more students will seek your help and want to write papers with you. Although departments may not always give you full credit for your work, I can promise you that the rewards will flow to you anyhow. Ultimately, papers and citations are counted in your professional standing, but people known to be good mentors have a lasting reputation of their own.

However, there may such a thing as *too* much generosity. Occasionally, faculty members are oblivious to whether they or their students are credited for common work. They work tirelessly to promote the success of their charges, sometimes even sacrificing their own professional standing. Perhaps these selfless individuals are doing just what they want. But these saints are few in number as far as I can tell. I would say that it is ill advised to give credit to a student if they are not deserving of it; it often comes back to haunt them if they have not actually done the work to merit the credit. Excessive generosity may actually not promote professional development but rather a sense of entitlement—not a good thing to foster.

Overall, the system probably works in the other direction. Senior figures more often underestimate student contributions, especially when the collaboration involves a prominent scholar and a student. Nonetheless, my impression—unsupported by any evidence that I was able to find—is that generally work relationships between faculty and students are not a chronic concern in academic life. I suspect that problematic situations arise relatively infrequently and not nearly as often as fictional accounts of academic life suggest. When they do occur, however, they are painful and traumatic for both parties. That is why they are often featured in popular descriptions of academic life.

As you enter midlife and beyond, keep in mind that professional reputation is not simply based on your scholarship. It rests in part on how you treat your colleagues and especially your students. Successful collaboration redounds to both parties and often creates a lasting bond between you and your students.

Part of the job of faculty members is to sponsor their able students by recommending them for the next step on the academic ladder—to graduate school, a postdoc, or for an academic position—or a job outside of academia. Over the course of a career, if you are like me, you will end up writing hundreds of these letters. A few words of advice from an old pro in letter writing.

First, try to avoid writing letters for people whom you cannot recommend with more than tepid enthusiasm. There is a well-understood code in academic life. Faint praise is damning, so try to write letters for people whom you can actually support. Describing someone as a capable researcher or saying that a thesis was competent is usually a death sentence for a student. Although it may be painful to reject someone, it is worse to write a disingenuous letter or to kill a candidate's chances of ever getting a job by writing a weak letter. Be honest both to the person who has asked for a recommendation. I've sometimes said to students that I have not worked with them closely enough to write a very strong letter. When I do write a recommendation, I try to be positive but honest, reserving superlatives to situations when I think they are deserved. I confess that I usually manage to find at least one area where a particular student is superior when I write letters of recommendation.

Letters can take a great deal of time or be quickly written in a fairly standard form. I've known colleagues who ask the students to write a draft of their own recommendations. I can't endorse this practice because it puts the student in a very uncomfortable position and can be misleading to those receiving the recommendation. But it is perfectly appropriate to ask the student for supporting materials if you need them. Some letters require a lot of time and care; others are more perfunctory, such as when a student needs support to get access to data. Make sure that your letter is proportionate to the purpose for which it is intended. For postdocs and appointments, you should be prepared to write more than a page because a detailed letter is generally taken more seriously and is likely to be more persuasive. As you move up the ranks, you will be asked to write letters for tenure or promotion decisions. Unless you know the candidate's work well, these requests require at least several days of work because you must read and review the candidate's work. I generally give a lot less attention to three-year reviews, if I do them at all.

It is okay to refuse to write letters in cases of promotion, but you must understand that it has consequences for the candidate. If letters are sent to sixteen experts for a promotion case and twelve of them refuse to write, it will probably adversely influence the candidate's chances of getting promoted. No one enjoys writing letters of recommendation unless you happen to count the student or colleague for whom you are writing as a good friend. But it is a professional duty that, I'm afraid, only grows over time. The academic system requires this sort of sponsorship. To shirk this responsibility or perform it carelessly undermines the integrity and credibility of the scholarly enterprise.

REVIEWING PAPERS AND PROPOSALS

Some departments may provide credit for editorial responsibilities or reviews, but most take it as a matter of course and give few rewards for this form of labor. I know people who refuse to do it, but most regard this kind of work as professional contributions, the dues of being a member of the academy. There is a lot of unpaid labor in academic life, and reviewing manuscripts, proposals, drafts of papers, and the like can easily consume the workday. This is yet another area of your job that requires time budgeting. There are several good reasons to accept the responsibilities of serving as a reviewer in addition to the obvious one of doing your duty to your discipline. The primary benefit is intellectual. You get a chance to preview work in your area of expertise long before it is published. You often become acquainted with fresh ideas and new data that may be relevant to your own scholarship. I often benefit from a review of literature in a related area in which I am doing research; it is an opportunity to discover work that you have not come across but need to read.

The downside is that reviews take time. Therefore, I accept reviews judiciously, reserving them for topics that coincide with work I am currently doing rather than work I have done in the past (unless I merely want to keep up with what is going on in that particular area). You can make your own rules, but it is fair to say no to requests that fall out of your field of expertise or simply because you have other reviews to do still in the pipeline. Don't overcommit and underperform just because it is easier to say yes than no. It does no favor to anyone for you to accumulate a pile of overdue reviews. It is far better to be conscientious and do fewer reviews than to take on more than you are able: do them well or not at all.

GOING TO CONFERENCES

In the list of professional activities that consume large amounts of time, I've saved the best for last—conference going. Professional conferences are activities that scholars either love or hate—or, for many of us, we both love and hate them at the same time. Yes, it is fun to go away and pal around with your friends from graduate school, meet new colleagues from elsewhere, and see the senior figures on parade. Some younger people, who can still burn the candle at both ends, regard professional conferences as providing a period of ritual license, where drinking and carousing late into the night is de rigueur. I'll admit it: early in my career, I was discovered asleep in a lounge chair next to the swimming pool of my hotel early in the morning after drinking a 32-ounce margarita in San Antonio. I can attest to the fact that conferences can foster social relationships.

Over time some of these pleasures begin to fade. As least they have for me as I have had to reckon the time and energy that conferences demand. Once I found myself in a beautiful conference site in Woods Hole on Cape Cod where I attended back-to-back meetings over a nine-day period with only a single day of relief between the two meetings. I hardly had time to get outside during the days and was far too tired to do anything but fall into bed when dinner ended. By the final couple of days, I was in such a state of crazed ill humor that I was barely civil to my colleagues at the second meeting. I had to apologize at one point, saying that I was in a state of Acute Conference Overload.

Nonetheless, I still allocate a large allowance in my schedule for professional meetings. These days I especially appreciate smaller ones where the intellectual exchange and flow of information is high. A lot of learning goes on in working conferences where papers are presented in intimate settings. This is where you can catch up on some of the most recent work in your field of expertise. It is also where you can present work in progress and get early and often essential feedback for papers or books in the works.

Annual disciplinary meetings can also be worthwhile. In the early part of your career, they are occasions to introduce yourself to your colleagues in your discipline. They are the best format for building a social network of friends and associates who share your scholarly interests. For younger scholars, they provide an opportunity to form or deepen relationships with senior scholars who may be critical to your advancement in the guild. By midlife these meetings continue to reinforce your professional bonds, but your interests may be shifting from promoting your own career prospects to advancing the careers of your students and younger colleagues.

I was trained in methods of survey research and sometimes find myself conducting informal surveys. (Important questions such as how many pairs of shoes did everyone bring to this meeting? Women carry more pairs on average, but over time they are beginning to converge with men!) I used to ask my fellow conferees about how many meetings of the last five that they had attended would they do over again? Based on my informal, non-random polling, it would appear that younger people find conferences more worthwhile than their older peers, or perhaps they simply have more energy for them. By midlife you will find yourself becoming a bit more discriminating because you realize that you are paying a higher price than you might have thought for the pleasures of intellectual exchange, comradeship, and travel. Being away becomes more disruptive to your work and family life. Bringing your family along, to be sure, can diminish the disruption even if it costs money. But you will find yourself caught between your desire to spend time with your colleagues and your family. The conference may be neither quite an effective way of doing business or of having a vacation.

Here are some ways that I have discovered to make conference going to large professional associations more useful and gratifying. Figure out which sessions you really need to attend and be there. If you are not benefiting from conference sessions, you should be asking yourself if you really needed to attend the meeting in the first place. Make appointments to see friends and former students rather than scheduling on the hoof. It is often desirable to schedule working meetings of a project group around conferences so that you are doing double duty and are able to save time that might otherwise be consumed by yet another trip. Whatever happens or does not happen at the larger meeting, you have not wasted the travel time.

Most of all, I advise using professional meetings as a way of motivating yourself to get papers done. This means that you should be writing a draft of the paper that you present before you go rather than leaving the writing for later. PowerPoint presentations make it simple for you to show an outline of a paper that may or may not have been written. My suggestion: Write the paper and *then* make the PowerPoint presentation, instead of just doing the PowerPoint show. If you follow this approach, you will be a lot closer to a finished product when you return from the meeting. Incidentally, this practice also helps discussants to do their job more effectively and provides you with useful critical feedback as they can read your paper in advance. Most meetings require written papers be given to discussants prior to the meeting, but these rules are frequently flouted. Using professional meetings as a deadline for drafting papers in progress will keep you on the road to productivity and promotion.

PROMOTION TO FULL PROFESSOR

Compared to the interminable discussions about tenure in academic life, rather little attention is given to the transition from associate to full professor. Like tenure, this transition typically occurs more swiftly and routinely in the sciences and is often protracted in the humanities. In the social sciences, depending on the field, this promotion can occur almost as fast as in the sciences (economics and sociology), or almost as slowly as in the humanities (anthropology and history when the latter field is included in the social sciences). Accordingly, promotion to full professor is regarded as a matter of course in some fields so long as productivity continues and as a new challenge for recognition in others. There are no reliable figures on the duration from associate to full professor. Roughly speaking, promotion can occur as quickly as five years or even less or it can take fifteen years or even more in some institutions. It undoubtedly occurs more swiftly in the sciences, where research is front-loaded in the early part of a professional career, than in the humanities, where knowledge is accumulated more slowly and the publication of books is required; as usual, the social sciences fall in between. Of course, there is huge variation depending on the institutional norms, the productivity of scholars, and the marketplace.

As I indicated in the beginning of this chapter, most academics quickly put the tenure process behind them and become, if anything, more productive in the decade afterward. When this happens, promotion almost inevitably occurs at a reasonable interval. Not infrequently, the occasion for promotion is prompted by an outside offer, but when departments are working well and have the backing of the administration, it should not require an outside offer to initiate promotion. How much work is enough and how much time is sufficient to merit a promotion? Local standards prevail, so it is best to understand how promotions to full professor are handled early on rather than waiting until you face the situation. It helps to have an understanding with your department chair and senior colleagues even before tenure about the requirements for promotion. But it is easy enough to examine the records of your senior colleagues to gauge the local norms.

Promotion involves another round of letters of recommendation. For many, this requirement presents no problems because your network of senior colleagues typically expands greatly after tenure and continues to grow as you conduct research and publish. What you want your reference letters to say when you come up for promotion is that you have continued to be productive and the scope of your research has expanded or deepened. In the top tier of research universities, it is sometimes said that you need to move from acquiring a national to an international reputation, but this is simply a way of saying that your work has attracted considerable notice and has some influence on your field. For the majority of readers, this will happen as a matter of course so long as you protect your time for research and writing and continue to invest in teaching. But I alluded to the problem facing a minority of academics as they move into midlife, losing interest or the motivation to do research after being awarded tenure or, like the colleague I mentioned earlier in the chapter, being diverted from research to administration.

If you find that you are not continuing to enjoy teaching or research during the first several years after tenure, it is important that you take stock of what you are telling yourself. It could be that you may be looking for a new and different challenge. While the evidence suggests that rather few academics leave teaching after receiving tenure, it nonetheless happens and sometimes for very good reasons. Some faculty members in midlife are drawn into administration; others decide that they want to move into the world of policy or action or find positions in the private sector; and a small minority simply become bored and disenchanted with academic life.

If you are among the disenchanted, just make sure that you do something about it and do not merely remain passively in place. Disaffected academics, who are sometimes referred to as "deadwood," are quickly marginalized by their colleagues. It is an uncomfortable, even intolerable, status in academia. If you feel that you are stuck, having invested years of your life in becoming an academic, and are not enjoying your life as a professor, don't become inert for too long, hoping that your feelings will pass. I can almost assure you that they will not go away unless you do something about them. There are many routes to reinvigorate your interests or to switch careers in midlife. In your mid-forties or even later in life, you can change directions. You really don't want to be spending the next twenty-five or even fifteen years riding it out.

CHANGING POSITIONS

One problem that you may be having in sustaining commitment is a poor fit between your interests and priorities and your current job. You like teaching, but it is not highly rewarded because your institution places such a high value on research or community service; or you like doing research, but you are at a place with a 3/3 teaching load or more. If you are in this position, do not linger too many years. Start looking for a new position, because it frequently takes some time to find a place that provides a better fit for your talents. The process of switching jobs requires some strategy on your part and a bit of good fortune in the marketplace.

Academics change jobs all the time, and a small minority of them are seemingly in an endless quest for the perfect position. The evidence on academic mobility suggests that most academics change jobs at least once during their lifetime.[13] "Going on the market," as it is sometimes referred to, is built into the structure of academic life. I observed in the very first chapter that very few people are initially able to find a position in a department as prestigious as the one they attended as a graduate student. This means that many productive academics tend to be on the lookout for a better job. Even when they are not, they are likely to be eventually asked to apply for positions at places that may want to recruit them. This is how the system works: people try to improve their circumstances, and departments are at the same time trying to change their rankings by recruiting influential and able scholars who will give them greater professional visibility. So discussing moving to another department is not like cheating on your partner, because loyalty in academia, even if it is desired in the abstract, is not expected in reality. Academics are encouraged to look around and see if they can improve their situation, and a few do so almost compulsively.

I can't say that I have ever found this particular feature of academic life appealing. But I've gotten used to seeing my colleagues come and go. You have to if you stay in one institution as I have done throughout my career. It is a way that departments become newly invigorated unless they merely are depleted, as sometimes occurs when administrations refuse to fill positions that have been vacated.

The main motivation for moving in many instances is not a strong discontent with present circumstances. To be sure, most academics can find a lot of things to complain about in their work life—teaching courses that they do not like, too many faculty meetings, too much administrative responsibility, an unenlightened administration, and the list goes on. These factors surely figure to some degree in decisions to move. But many academics, especially those who continue to publish, perceive rightly that they can improve their salary and work conditions by moving on and preferably up. There is a widespread perception that if you don't test the market at least occasionally, you are doing yourself a personal disservice. This perception, I'm afraid, is probably correct at least when it comes to salary increases. Many times it is nearly impossible to get a raise above the rate of inflation unless you have a competing offer. Thus, professors who are relatively satisfied with their position, if not their pay, are tempted to go on the market.

Especially if you are discontent with your position, but even if you are not, it is likely that you will find yourself thinking about going on the market. If you feel as though you are being poorly treated or under-appreciated for what you do, underpaid, and overworked, you should try to move. And there are other reasons that have little to do with your own circumstances. You may need to move for a host of other reasons that might improve your life. You like the outdoors and you got tenure at a city university or vice versa. Your partner can't find a good job in the small college town that you are living in. And so on.

I would be less keen on moving just for a modest salary increase or the promise of a larger research fund if you are happy where you are. There are a lot of hidden costs to moving. Most of all, it is highly disruptive and takes a lot of time to settle in to a new institution. More-over, if you think that you can escape departmental responsibilities, you will often be wrong. There is a not insignificant chance that you will suffer buyer's remorse, wishing that you had remained in the com-munity where your children were happy or your partner had a better job. So take care as you contemplate moving to consider if you will ac-tually improve your situation and be more content in the next position than you are in the one that you presently hold.

An academic acquaintance of mine, who has difficulty regulating his workload, seems to move every five years or so, because he tires of all the committee work and student dissertations. Much of this work he seems to leave behind for others to clean up when he moves to an-other place. His reputation now precedes him. He is always sanguine that the next department that he joins will come with fewer obliga-tions. Gradually, his colleagues are catching on, and his mobility may be hampered in time. But I am afraid this is how it sometimes works for academic stars.

A few suggestions on managing a mid-career move: First, be clear in your own mind, before reentering the job market, what you want to get from changing places. Doing this helps you decide whether the grass will really be greener or just the same slightly mottled color that it is where you live. Second, never threaten your colleagues or administra-tion that you are planning to leave without a better offer in hand, unless you are absolutely certain that they don't want you to go. Life will probably become worse if you threaten to leave and stay, unless you are widely appreciated. So keep your fantasies of the next job to yourself (or your close friends) until you actually have an alternative position in hand. Never shadow bargain or try bluffing your way into a salary increase or some other benefit by threatening to go if you don't get it. If you haven't gotten the rewards that you feel are merited, feel free to complain but don't threaten to leave merely as a bargaining tactic unless you are prepared to go. Get a good job offer and then begin your negotiations if you must. But understand that you must be prepared to leave if your offer is not matched. Your credibility will plummet if you are bluffing.

A former colleague threatened to leave almost on an annual basis unless he got a substantial raise. He did this several times, and it paid off handsomely because he was an attractive figure on the job market. But he was taken up short in the end when the administration finally told him that he should accept the better offer he had kept alive for a number of years. To this day, I do not know if he really wanted to leave, but leave he did after being told that his bargaining days were over.

Apply the same level of due diligence in considering outside offers as advised in earlier chapters. Do not let your fantasies of the next place replace the reality of how things might actually turn out. If you are reasonably happy where you are, but just might be better off at another spot, consider visiting there on leave or sabbatical before giving up your present job. If your colleagues and administration want you to stay, a leave of absence is almost always possible. If it seems too disruptive to move for a year or two, consider how disruptive it could be if you move and are not happy in your new position.

Serial movers often earn a bad reputation in academia. They may receive higher salaries and better work conditions as they advance from place to place, but if they appear to be simply chasing the goodies, it does not serve their overall professional standing. As you consider moving, think about whether you are prepared to make at least a five-year commitment to your new position. If you are not, think about whether this new job is the right one for you. Academic life works best when faculty members are committed to their departments and their students. Academic stars are most appreciated when they share the collective interests of their departments. When they are considered as free agents, acting primarily in their own interests, they are treated with a certain amount of circumspection by their colleagues and students because no one really expects them to be around for very long.

THE CHALLENGES OF ACADEMIC MIDLIFE

The second third of academic life is a lot easier to manage than the first third especially if you are fortunate enough to get into a good groove— that is, find a position where you get along and respect your colleagues and can attract able students. You have mastered the skills of your discipline but are reaching to expand them. You become more confident in your ability to pick interesting problems to work on, and your work is well received in your profession. Most academics in midlife are quite satisfied in their jobs, even if they are somewhat less so than their younger or more senior colleagues, owing to the greater job demands that they must contend with.[14]

I would be remiss not to say something about those who cannot manage to find a congenial department in which they can hang their hat and must settle for something far less than what they had hoped to accomplish by midlife. According to the surveys of full-time or even part-time academics, these individuals represent a distinct minority. By mid-career many discontented academics have left the system for alternate careers. Other midlife academics have learned to be satisfied enough where they are to appreciate the benefits of doing what they like to do most—teaching and research. They have come to believe that the glass is full enough for them. Perhaps as many as a quarter of the readers of this chapter, however, are still hoping to improve their circumstances because their position is not "good enough." My advice to them is to keep trying, because many will indeed find a better position in time.

But to those of you who are becoming bitter and cynical about the rewards of academic life, who really wish that they never had to face another class of undergraduates or present another paper at a professional meeting, I say to you that life is too short to feel that you are wasting your time in academic life. If at all possible, find something different to do. You'll probably only get more disaffected over time if you lose the passion that brought you into academic life in the first place.

I give these words of advice understanding full well that academia does not work out for everyone. The rewards of being a professor are unevenly—and I for one would say unfairly—divided between those at the top tiers and those at the bottom tiers of colleges and universities. It is harder to feel appreciated at a bottom-tier university, a struggling college, or an underfunded community college because you are less rewarded in these positions, certainly when it comes to extrinsic benefits. Yet surveys show that most individuals are quite satisfied in less prestigious locations in academic society because they value their work and hence value their life in academia.[15] I am *not* suggesting the discontented should merely pull their socks up and learn to be satisfied with what they have. To the contrary, I am saying if you are not content with what you have accomplished with your PhD by midlife, you should be considering alternatives. It is still not too late to make a change either to a place that provides a better fit for you or to a nonacademic position. Don't stay in place and grow angrier, because this strategy is bound to fail.

5

THE ENDGAME

Seniority in academic life has two distinct meanings: first, it is the major step on the academic ladder after an untenured or junior faculty member receives tenure and becomes senior faculty with full rights and privileges. This move to seniority typically happens early in midlife, though its timing depends on the discipline, university, and pace of productivity. Seniority in this sense has to do with power and responsibility associated with tenure (or its equivalent in systems that may not have a formal tenure process). There are other ways of conferring senior status, such as being vested in a pension plan or being designated as a senior lecturer or an adjunct professor.

The second meaning of seniority is colloquial and much more subjective. I use the term to refer to the later stage of an academic's life or, roughly speaking, the last third of an academic career. Based on a psychological clock and a social timetable derived through experience and longevity, it is both an internal state of mind and a social reality. A sense of seniority generally occurs when professors begin to reckon with the aging process and contemplate concluding their academic career. No doubt, some readers who are in their late fifties, sixties, or even seventies reading this sentence may be saying to themselves: "I will never retire. I love what I am doing, and they will have to carry me out of here!" Don't be concerned if you feel this way: I will reserve part of the chapter for a discussion of these feelings, because I have a lot of sympathy with your point of view. But it is not the way a vast majority of older academics actually behave or even feel as they approach the endgame.

Years ago, when I was still a young professor, I was invited to be a member of a review committee for the sociology department at a distinguished university. At one point in our visit, the chair of the department introduced our committee to a group of tenured associate professors, all of whom were in their forties, as "junior faculty" who would eventually be the next generation of leadership. Indeed, none of them had an active role in the running of the department because leadership was exclusively reserved for a handful of senior members who were a couple of decades older than the associate professors in the department. The absence of younger "senior" faculty in positions of responsibility in the department shocked members of the review committee and was duly noted in our report. Just a few years later, the department was being managed more equitably and incidentally had become more prominent in the process. Unlike what occurs in most medical schools, academic departments are not generally run as gerontocracies with the power being vested in one strong leader who is very senior.

Indeed, I think it is fair to say that age per se earns you very little in academic life. Younger faculty members are often paid more than older ones in a tenure system (though not always in a system governed by union rules) because they have more years of a productive career ahead of them and are potentially more mobile. As I described in the last chapter, it is common for younger academics to try to improve their circumstances by moving to a better position with greater benefits. Sometimes I have been asked if there is an age when you become too old to be attractive on the job market. Technically speaking, there is no such age, but in reality very few departments recruit senior members once they are in their sixties. It happens but usually only occurs among academics who have an outstanding record of continued productivity or who are being hired because they offer unique assets to another department.

A friend of mine at a well-known university reported that the dean made it clear to her that the administration would look unfavorably on hiring faculty in their fifties. Of course, what he was telling her was illegal, but his views, no doubt, framed the hiring decisions at the university. Based on personal observation, it may work a little differently in some European countries, especially Mediterranean countries, where age and a long track record are given a bit more weight. This seems paradoxical, because the United States has no mandatory retirement age while most European countries do. Perhaps the disparity is due to the fact that few disciplines in the natural and social sciences believe that senior figures are as likely to produce cutting-edge work as younger academics. Hiring decisions in the United States probably take years of future productivity into account *because* of the absence of a retirement age.

This view of academic productivity, whether fully warranted or not, tends to influence how academics feel as they enter their sixties, when most begin to experience some of the conspicuous signs of aging that are familiar to all of us both inside and outside of academia. Of course, these signs begin much earlier in life: students appear younger and younger with the passing years. Even in our twenties, undergraduates first appear to us like younger siblings. Assistant professors not infrequently find themselves hanging out with their graduate students. But before you know it, students become the ages of our children, and you are more likely to tend to them rather than to hang out with them. How well I remember a couple of decades ago, when I was in midlife, giving a lecture to a group of medical interns and realizing to my horror that they were truly a younger generation than I. At such moments, we all wish that we could slow down the clock. Most senior academics can attest to the fact that the perception of time passing actually speeds up as you get older. It seemed like it was only a short time ago when I was beginning the final third of my academic career, but of late I have been playing my own version of the endgame.

Retirement is a difficult and even delicate subject in the United States because ours is a society that values work and productivity so highly that exiting gainful employment when you are still capable of earning income, at least for many professionals, feels like social death. Most of the discussions in the academic literature on retirement concern the economics of leaving the labor market—an important consideration to be sure but hardly the sole consideration for many of us. This final chapter will discuss the options and alternative ways of managing the last third of an academic career, especially the process of phasing down and eventually moving out of academia. But let's not start in the final decade of academic life for most professors—the sixties—but rather the first decade of seniority before most academics even face the decision of whether or when to give up their position.

While full professors frequently complain, usually with good reason, that they have too much to do, it is typically a satisfying time of professional life for most of us. The majority enters a sweet spot in their career at midlife, as I noted in the previous chapter, which typically continues well into the last third of their academic careers. Responsibilities continue to increase, but skills and appetite for work generally are high in the senior ranks. New challenges are often self-imposed, whether it is a more ambitious research project or teaching new courses that involve mastering new knowledge that can result in a different stream of scholarly work. I'll come to these often-welcome challenges in a moment, but first let's discuss the less appealing features of seniority, the proverbial need to "eat your spinach."

The biggest and often most time-consuming activities are administrative or organizational. The burdens of department responsibilities necessarily fall upon senior professors. You will have a hard time dodging the responsibilities of running things. And running things, as we have seen in earlier chapters, involves a host of duties ranging from chairing the department to running the graduate or undergraduate program, recruiting new faculty, or organizing the admission of students. A few professors will evade these responsibilities or do them so poorly that they will not be asked again after demonstrating incompetence, but there is strong normative pressure from colleagues and administration to pull your weight.

The housekeeping duties seem endless. It is amazing how much time can be consumed in helping a foreign student to adjust to the peculiarities of American-style academic life or dealing with how to reassign the classes of a colleague who faces a serious illness. Small crises are consistently popping up that demand the attention of the senior faculty.

And then there are the meetings. Like grading papers, I'm not sure that I've met an academic who *enjoys* going to faculty meetings. Because decisions are typically made collaboratively (at least among senior faculty), meetings are endemic to academic life. They are the source of parody in fiction because of their distinctive style. Most faculty members expect to have their say, and so they do. Efficiency of decision making among academics is not a virtue widely observed. Rather, we academics are inclined to encourage an open-throated discussion of issues—even minor reforms in the curriculum or whether or not to open a graduate student workshop to interested undergraduates. Dissent is widely countenanced if not encouraged. It is no exaggeration to say that many academics prefer to speak in paragraphs rather than sentences.

Many senior academics complain that too much time is taken up by committee work and administrative duties. The fact is that it is difficult to run operations by committee. My impression is that departments work best when there is intelligent delegation along with ample consultation. But that requires a level of trust in the wisdom of a good chair and hardworking colleagues who know when to bring an issue to the full faculty for discussion and when not to. Trust of colleagues is a commodity that in some departments is in short supply. Faculty members get involved in relatively small and inconsequential decisions because they are often unwilling to delegate authority to their colleagues.

As I have observed in earlier chapters, departments vary tremendously in the degree of collegiality evidenced. It's a lot more work to be in a department where people do not get along. When senior faculty members are in conflict, the side costs to everyone—students, staff, and faculty members alike—are higher than when there is some measure of harmony and cooperation.

Early in my life at Penn, there was so much infighting in my department that we were put into receivership by the provost. It took some time and a lot of energy to right things to the point where we were permitted to run our own affairs again. My experience as a young professor was probably more the exception than the rule, I must add. While a lot of complaining goes on about the behavior of colleagues, generally departments govern themselves adequately if not often with a high degree of skill or efficiency. But they cannot do so without the strong involvement of the senior faculty. I said in the introduction that governance must be shared. If there is widespread opting out by senior professors or, alternatively, if they are permitted to run the show completely, expect there to be problems in the departmental climate.

By this stage in an academic career, most faculty members know how to multitask. As I have discussed in earlier chapters, if you are to stay the course in academic life, you must be able to find sufficient time for what nourishes you. That may be teaching or research; it is probably both for most readers in varying degrees. No more talk in this final chapter of schedules and maintaining the discipline of working on the research projects that sustain many of us in academic life. If you don't have the discipline by now, you probably are not going to acquire it during the final third of your career.

The new challenge that you face in this stage of your career is not so much in how to get things done, but rather in how to keep your work life fresh and exciting. It is essential to maintain the sense of wonderment, delight, and curiosity of discovering new ideas and approaches to your work that you have experienced earlier in your academic life. Without that sense of fascination—often accompanied by a mild obsession that you are working on something important—you can easily become disenchanted in the latter stages of your academic career. Disenchantment with what drew you into academic life—love of ideas and the production of new knowledge—can be deadly, because it casts an evil spell on both research and teaching and breeds cynicism about your colleagues and students.

I could find little research and not even much discussion on how academics fare during this stage of life. It appears that teaching effectiveness is not strongly related to age, but there is some evidence that research productivity tends to decline slightly beginning sometime in the fifties. Even if true—and it has not been well or widely established—these aggregate figures are not very informative about what drives the average downward.[1] In any case, the overall decline is slight, leaving open the more important question of who thrives and who does not. And, more to the point for readers of this book, there is little discussion of how to maintain if not increase a sense of commitment in the final decade or two of teaching. Here is my take on how to manage senior status.

Getting good at something like teaching or research and writing takes a long time for most of us. Of course, you can always get better at what you do. Some of us never hit a speed bump and just go on finding new challenges in our academic careers. I wrote about this in the previous chapter and have little more to say to readers who just love what they are doing and want to do it as long as they are able. Most of my colleagues and friends are in this category: they are still in love with their jobs as they reach their senior years. Of course, this is far easier to manage if you are in the ranks of the privileged. The challenges of maintaining commitment are likely much greater in the lower tiers of academia, where work conditions can be grueling and extrinsic rewards are far less generous. Even so, surveys indicate that most academics in later life retain a high satisfaction with their work life. The differences in job satisfaction at the top and bottom tiers are far less than I would have imagined before consulting the data. Many of us seem to like what we are doing and are more than willing to continue in our academic career, even when we are not rewarded well monetarily or showered with the perks that are standard fare in the most prestigious colleges and universities.[2]

Even among contented academics, it is critical to refresh what you are doing by taking on new projects inside and outside of the classroom. Approaching the age of fifty, I had never had a sabbatical outside of Philadelphia. Spending more time away from the university, as I began to do in my fifties, exposed me to new opportunities for research and new ideas to enrich my teaching. It helped me avoid the feeling of becoming stale and bored. Sabbaticals—the time-honored practice of stepping out of everyday academic life—can be a godsend, and they are certainly among the most appealing features of academia. But sabbaticals are not available to all academics and probably will become scarcer if the present climate of austerity continues. Many senior academics can afford, as they become more financially secure, to use their summers as a short sabbatical, developing projects that take them far afield to invigorate their research and teaching.

My point here is pretty obvious: it is critical not to become routinized as you reach the final third of your academic career. If you don't continue to grow intellectually, it will be reflected in your teaching and research. You will probably feel it before others notice it, but be assured that they will in time notice it, even if you don't. So you must plan for a certain amount of reinvention of yourself as you enter seniority. This is not as difficult as it may seem; many academics do this continuously as they venture into new areas of teaching and research. But if you are giving the same lectures year after year and writing slight variations of the same ideas, I can almost guarantee that you will be discontent with how you feel as you age in academia.

A certain number of faculty—and I know of no data to document just how many there are—fall into a rut after scaling the academic ladder. They don't enjoy doing the same things, such as teaching a course that used to excite them or preparing conference papers for meetings that they have been attending for twenty-five or thirty years. No wonder, if they have done these things many times before, they are simply not as interesting to do again and again. Of course, as I noted in previous chapters, there are pathways out of the same-old, same-old. Administration is perhaps the most common way of doing something different—at least for a while. There are other options, such as consulting or community ventures, that may provide welcome sources of stimulation, but it is important to recognize if these activities are designed and motivated to enrich your academic life or whether they are pathways of escaping from the reality of being dissatisfied with teaching or doing research or even helping to facilitate others doing so.

If you are beginning to feel this way, push yourself to teach a new course. Tackle a problem that you feel unprepared to take on without a lot of new knowledge. Break a boundary in your discipline. This is the time of life to take some chances, like applying for a Fulbright, learning a new language, or launching a new program in your community. The prospects for doing something different or unusual abound in academic life. Even if your new fantasies are not completely realized, you are likely to reap some benefits of having the fantasies. In other words, don't let the gray matter grow too gray because it doesn't feel good if you are surrounded by younger colleagues brimming with energy and enthusiasm while you are stagnating.

After more than four decades in the business, I have watched a lot of academics grow older. Now I am one of them. What I have learned is that the best antidote to becoming bored is described in the previous chapter as "generativity," Erik Erikson's term for an ability to mentor and an interest in investing in the development of younger people.[3] Academics who have the capacity to give to others never seem to lose enthusiasm for their work. These folks enjoy being around younger people, they are interested in their ideas and perceptions, they like providing advice and assistance, and they enjoy collaborating with students and younger faculty. They continue to give us the sense that they are having fun in their jobs.

The opposite approach to becoming more generative in the later years of academic life is hazardous; its absence often creates problems for academics in later life. Older academics who talk obsessively about their past contributions to their discipline, how things were more difficult when they were coming up, how there are no important ideas in their field these days—let's face it—become tedious to their peers and often boring to their students. Academics who want to hold on to their privileges even when they are no longer justified are understandably resented by their younger colleagues.

I think sadly about a colleague in a related discipline—I'll call him Henry—who hardly ever did a thing for anyone when he was in his prime. He was known in his department for always gaming the system to his advantage. Henry complained about his salary, the size of his office, and the lack of appreciation for his research contributions. He rarely attracted students, and when he did, they found that they did not want to work with him because he was frequently trying to get them to do research for his current projects. Henry didn't lose interest in his work, but he gradually became more isolated from his colleagues because he simply refused to help out with the committee work. He was forced to retire because he reached the age of seventy before the Supreme Court decision in 1994 that affirmed legislation in the previous decade overturning mandatory retirement among tenured academics. Henry wanted to continue teaching in his department, but he had never been willing and able to work closely with undergraduates. His department refused his request. His lack of generosity and concern for his colleagues eventually caught up to him, and I am sorry to say that he died an embittered man.

Contrast Henry's not completely uncommon experience with an acquaintance of mine at another university who had been a well-known scholar in his prime and continued to contribute to his field until he retired. Fred loved academic life, being around students, and helping out. I last saw Fred when he was nearing eighty. His department continued to provide an office for him. By all accounts, I was told that Fred was besieged by students and colleagues who valued his wisdom, enjoyed his tales of the early days of research in his field, and appreciated his willingness to read and comment on their papers. Fred was esteemed as much as Henry was spurned in his older years.

As I observed in the previous chapter, generativity comes more easily if it is a pattern that is adopted earlier in your career. If you liked the role of mentoring and appreciated the success of your students when you were younger, in all likelihood you will not have problems in the final third of your academic career. If you remain enthusiastic about teaching and continue to enjoy contact with your students, the prognosis for adjusting to your later decades is good. And if research and writing continue to give you a thrill, as it does for me, you are not likely to have a difficult time as you approach retirement. To put it in its simplest terms, I would say that if you do not still feel a sense of play when you reach the later years of your career, you may be telling yourself that you should alter your work habits or perhaps call it quits.

It is not easy to shift your lifelong patterns as you enter the final decade of your academic career. In my experience, it really is necessary for most of us, however much we remain professionally visible and vital. Call it what you will, but I like to think of it as a capacity to shrink your ego, lower your expectations (and especially demands) for extrinsic rewards, and devote more of your time to assisting others in getting their work done. It can be lots of fun, just as being a grandparent is, but this shift in work orientation requires an internal recalibration for those of us who are used to being front and center stage. Many readers will not find this difficult while for others it may be a huge challenge, especially for men of my generation whose professional identity is often the single egg in their basket.

I hasten to add that this pattern of giving need not interfere with your own academic accomplishments. It is just that your name does not always need to be first on papers. You do not always need to lead a project unless it will be helpful to do so. Most of all, if you were not so inclined before now, it becomes more important to give someone else the lion's share of the credit. At about the time that I turned sixty, I made a rule for myself: I would no longer be the first author on any paper that I did with someone younger than myself—virtually everyone with whom I was likely to collaborate. It was an easy rule to follow, and I do not think it affected my professional standing at all. Indeed, it made me a more attractive collaborator, and I usually managed to avoid doing some of the more tedious work on a project or paper I often had to do in my younger years. This meant that I could take on more students in collaborative research. Of course, I continued to write sole-authored books and articles because I had more time to do so.

CONTEMPLATING RETIREMENT

Remarkably little is written about the retirement *process* in an academic life. Just as I began to write this chapter, I was asked to respond to a survey on this topic, and it will be interesting to see the findings when they appear. But for the most part, I cannot rely much on hard evidence about the retirement process for academics apart from studies of timing and financial evaluations. There are not even very many reflections or accounts in the academic trade journals.[4] So I am flying partially blind in the discussion that follows of how professors manage the retirement process, depending more on my own observations than I have in earlier chapters, where there is voluminous evidence and observations in the academic literature.

As any reader of this book will know by now, I am by nature a planner. I began to think about retirement a decade before I faced the decision. But I recognize that not many of my friends and colleagues are like me. They considered me slightly peculiar for thinking about giving up my position long before I really needed to and while still enjoying my work. Most academics, like me, holding an attractive job prefer not to think about giving up their tenured position and the many perks that are provided to tenured faculty before they really feel their powers flagging. Most of all, they reason, perhaps correctly: Why stop getting paid for what you enjoy doing? This is a good question, and I will return to it shortly.

All but a tiny minority of academics formally retire somewhere between their early sixties and early seventies.[5] The evidence suggests that in less favorable circumstances—below the first and second tiers of academic institutions—faculty are more willing to contemplate retirement earlier probably because they pay a much higher price for continuing to work in their jobs. Many are overworked and underpaid, and they look forward to a change of pace and perhaps a change of place. It depends on if they can afford it, the available institutional supports, and whether they have a plan for what they might do when they stop being a full-time academic. But they see retirement as freedom to work as they wish to or do something altogether different—if they can afford to stop.

I will not delve into detail about the economics of retirement in this book. The vast majority of academics who have held tenure-track positions will be in a good position to make the decision of whether and when to retire largely on non-economic grounds. But in the bottom tiers of academic life, retirement benefits can be ungenerous. There are, no doubt, some readers who really cannot afford to retire when they might otherwise prefer to do so. This is especially true for aging adjuncts who have always pieced together a living by teaching at several institutions. We should know more than we do about how those in the secondary labor market of academia manage as senior adjuncts. The following discussion assumes that you have reasonable benefits and are therefore in a position to decide whether or not to continue in your post on non-pecuniary grounds.

Recently, I attended the annual professional meeting of the Population Association of America (PAA), which is attended by demographers, sociologists, economists, and a handful of those from other disciplines who study issues related to population. I have been going to this conference for years, and, like all such meetings, you immediately run into longtime friends, former students, and colleagues from other universities. Since I have been writing this book, these sorts of meetings provide an opportunity for doing fieldwork of sorts. My interest this time was talking to my older friends about their thoughts on retirement.

Within a matter of minutes of cruising across the lobby of the conference hotel, I ran into a colleague from another university who was in his early sixties. When I asked him about his retirement plans, he told me, "I just cannot wait to retire. I have so many things that I want to do." He had lost interest in research and found that teaching had become routine. He was beginning to count the days before he could spend more time traveling, gardening, reading, and getting more involved in political life in his community. He had enjoyed his time as an academic but no longer felt inspired by his work. His wife, a more visible academic, was not so sure about how she felt about stopping as early as he planned to. As far as he was concerned, it was her choice when to retire. He was ready and eager to stop.

The next person I ran into had been a former officer in the PAA. He was almost a decade older than I, but he was still teaching and actively involved in his department. "I am going to die with my boots on if I possibly can," he told me. He was in excellent shape and looked like he had a number of fruitful years ahead of him.

These two extremes of opinion and everything in between have been voiced in conversations that I've had with senior academics in settings like the PAA over the past several years: we all begin academic life in a pretty similar way, as I described in the first chapter of this book. Graduate departments and programs vary in subtle and important ways, but they offer a common experience that is not too difficult to summarize. Exiting academia is more varied because it is not as tightly regulated by institutional rules, strong incentives, and established norms for stepping down.

Explaining the variation requires, as the two above cases illustrate, that we delve into differences in personal preferences, satisfaction with current job conditions, alternative options for work and play, family circumstances, financial conditions, and a host of other factors that figure into how academic careers are concluded. It is necessary to take all of the conditions into account if we are to understand how we academics think about and manage retirement. For purposes of the discussion of these options, it is useful to bundle them into three general patterns that academics often take as they reach the latter part of their careers: The most common pattern is to cut the cord that binds them to their position swiftly and retire as soon as it is economically feasible; at the other extreme, a far smaller number of academics chose to stay in place as long as they are physically able to do so; and the third alternative, which may be becoming a more prevalent one, is to phase out gradually.

CUTTING THE CORD

Making a living as an academic has an awful lot of advantages, as I have stressed repeatedly throughout this book. Many of us get to do what we most like: thinking, learning, telling others about what we have learned, and investing in younger people, along with a certain dash of travel—often to interesting places to do interesting things. Yet the composition of our work varies greatly depending on the position that we have been able to get. It is hard to deny that the gap between the haves and the have-nots is as great in academia as it is elsewhere in our society. Some of us make a lot more money and have a lot more latitude in how we earn it than others. Indeed, many academics must endure working conditions that make what we do less fun or not fun at all.

Academic life, good as it is, can be onerous even under the best of conditions. Under the worst of conditions—when teaching loads are crushing, administrative duties are tedious, and department life is unrewarding—retirement seems like the rational thing to do even if it comes with some apprehensions about "giving up your status," as people sometimes describe it. This is probably the reason that the vast majority of academics are ready to call it quits when they reach the normative age of retirement in the United States—somewhere between sixty-five and seventy for professionals—especially when they have a reasonable pension or nest egg.[6]

Some subset of those who give up their academic position—I could find no good supportive evidence on just how large it is—actually does not really stop working when they "retire." Many academics who step down from a tenured position or something like tenure where they have earned a high level of job security do so in order to complete the book that they never had an opportunity to finish or undertake a research project for which they never could get funding. These freelancers, if they can afford it, are happy just to do the work that gave them reason to become an academic, but at their own pace and without anyone looking over their shoulder to see if they are being productive in a gainful sense. They are not retiring because they have to but because they want to and are willing to forgo added income for freedom from oversight and participation in many of the less pleasant aspects of academic life. Strange as it may seem, these senior scholars want to go on working, but they prefer to do it on their own time. And some believe, as I do, that academic life requires a faculty turnover to reinvigorate institutions.

I have mentioned the reasons for retiring even when you want to go on working as a scholar: you can peel off parts of the job that almost no one likes, such as administrative work, showing up for faculty meetings, unrewarding classes, grading exams, and the like. But it is important to recognize the drawbacks of retirement. In certain departments, giving up your title will, no doubt, be accompanied by a certain amount of disregard by colleagues. Your opinion may not count any longer: your influence over which students are admitted disappears, policies that you have advocated may be changed, and students may ignore you if they know that you are no longer a member of the standing faculty. I can't say that this never happens, so take a good look at how retired members of your department are treated before you make any final decision.

Most institutions provide an honorable, even attractive, way of stepping down these days.[7] They often award their faculty an honorary position, professor emeritus, which provides a title if not always an office and a continued presence in the department. Many departments both allow and encourage their faculty to teach on an occasional basis. Increasingly, institutions that can afford to try to make life after service attractive by involving emeriti faculty in departmental roles that may involve advising students, providing help to junior faculty, and the like. Fred, whom I admiringly wrote about earlier, no longer receives a salary, but he feels very much a part of his department.

But as I've already said, a large (but unknown) proportion of retirees from academia retire in order to do something else and have little or no interest in hanging around. They may begin another job doing something altogether different, take up a longtime avocation, engage in community activities, care for their grandchildren, or even just enjoy life in the slow lane.

There was a time—before 1994—when almost all professors *had* to retire by the age of seventy. Then the Supreme Court affirmed congressional legislation passed in 1986, abolishing mandatory retirement for tenured professors, leaving the decision of when to retire up to individuals. It created the kind of "natural experiment" that economists love to study. Two prominent economists examined how the change in the law affected the age of retirement.[8] Not surprisingly, it did make a difference: more academics continued to work into their seventies after the Supreme Court decision than before it. However, the distribution of retirement ages shifted only slightly. A somewhat higher proportion of academics began to delay retirement until their early seventies, but the increase was smaller than many predicted and some feared. And, mostly, academics work longer when they are well compensated and do not have too great a workload. Retirement is a bit later in the top-tier schools than at lower rungs on the prestige ladder. Predictably, earlier retirement also occurs when faculty feel financially secure, so the timing depends on the package of support accumulated over years of service. Considering that most top-tier schools have a very good package, retirement would probably come even later in the more prestigious institutions were it not for the fact that the law requires that individuals start drawing from their tax-deferred retirement funds by the age of seventy.

As I said, most readers of this chapter who are in the endgame will be ready to cut the cord by their late sixties and nearly all by their early seventies. But it is well to do some thinking and planning before you come to this point. Almost everyone in the course of academic life witnesses faculty retiring. Watch your reactions as you enter your senior years. It is not difficult to sense how you feel about the idea of retirement. But if it fills you with terror, it is surely a sign that you need to do some serious thinking about it. One of my friends told me recently: "I don't want to think about it. I know that I have to face the decision soon, but I just keep putting it out of my mind." Maybe his strategy of denial will work for him, but it seems obvious that individuals who do not have alternative ways of getting satisfaction from their lives other than through work may be playing a reckless endgame. Workaholics be aware and study carefully the next section of this chapter.

STAYING IN PLACE

I have a friend, Robert, who confessed to me some years ago as he was approaching his eighth decade that he was sure that he would never retire. "I love what I am doing—why should I ever stop?" Robert told me. I asked him, "But how do your colleagues feel about your plans?" He initially appeared a bit nonplussed by the question but seemed sure that they were very supportive. To be fair to Robert, I knew from other conversations that his colleagues were more than willing to have him stay in the department as he entered his seventies. He was still continuing to hold up his end of the bargain. My question to him was more rhetorical because I suspected that Robert would face a time in the next five years when his colleagues would be less happy about having him continue to teach full-time in a small department that needed younger hires. Sure enough, five years later everyone that I knew in his department was contriving of ways to get Robert to give up his professorship, but he still did not realize that he was regarded with less favor than had once been the case. Robert continued to write, even though his work no longer appeared in prominent places; along with this, his students dwindled and his colleagueship was no longer as respected as it had once been. The last person to know was Robert, because he really did not want to know.

Let me be clear: research on longevity in the labor force indicates that tremendous variation exists in patterns of aging, especially among professionals whose energy and appetite for work remains stronger than blue-collar laborers and service workers who do relatively routine or physically demanding jobs. Some academics can continue to pull their weight beyond their early seventies. Their writings remain crisp and cutting edge. Their teaching is inspiring, and students rush to work with them for fear that they may miss out on the opportunity. And their colleagues will go to great lengths to keep them around.

One of my closest friends is just such a person. Now past the age of seventy, Linda is still doing it all. She has high visibility in her research, an uncanny ability to run things, and is also by all accounts a gifted teacher. Her partner wants her to stop, but she is just having too much fun. She tells me that she is planning to phase down in a couple of years, and while I am not sure that she will be really ready to taper off, there is no doubt in my mind that Linda will stop when she is not giving more than she is getting in her position. However, I expect her to continue working on at least a part-time basis for another five years or more.

In my academic life, I have known a small number of professors who have continued to do very good work in their fields well into their eighties. Eleanor Maccoby, the prolific developmental psychologist, was still doing interesting work when she reached ninety. The same goes for my good friend Howard Becker, a fellow sociologist in his mid-eighties, even though he formally retired more than a decade ago. Matilda Riley, an expert on aging herself, was going strong until she was almost ninety. And there are others—probably many more in the humanities and social sciences than in the natural sciences—who continue to write and teach until the end of their lives or at least until their health fails them.

There is a lot of individual variation in the longevity of work life. Culturally, we know that social timetables are quite variable. Benjamin Franklin, an academic of sorts, regarded himself as "elderly" in his late fifties, although he ended up living an immensely creative and productive life for almost three more decades. As the baby boom generation likes to believe, seventy today might feel more like sixty in another few decades. In any case, not everyone follows the same schedule of aging, owing to important biological and psychological differences.

My impression, however, is that there are more Roberts—academics who put off retiring beyond the age that they should in the view of their colleagues—than Lindas, academics who can stay on and are appreciated by their colleagues and students. It is very hard to know when to stop if you like what you are doing and do not have a lot of alternatives that are as fun and rewarding as staying in place. Besides, it is difficult to give up a six-figure salary, even if your work is not quite as fun and rewarding as Linda finds it.

Over the years, I have given a lot of thought about how to know when it is time to stop. My conclusion is that it is almost impossible for professors to make that sort of judgment reliably because we academics are inclined to overestimate our contributions to our institutions and often lack the ability to perceive how our colleagues see our respective contributions. Don't count on your friends and colleagues to tell you it is time to retire: it simply won't happen. For one reason, telling you that you are less capable of doing your job because you are getting older is against the law, so the issue of retirement is treated delicately in most institutions. In any case, younger friends and colleagues are disinclined to tell you the truth even if you ask them directly.

Here are a few indicators that you should consider if you want to stay on into your seventies. First, look at your scholarly work. Are you as productive and creative as you were in your prime? Or perhaps a more forgiving standard is whether you are still in the top half of your department in scholarly accomplishment. Second, are your teaching evaluations above average for your department? Third, are you still holding up your end of the bargain when it comes to doing departmental housework? Perhaps the clearest sign is an internal one: are you beginning to slack off even if no one else knows? If the fear of retirement—due to lack of an attractive alternative or the need to hold on to your position for your psychological well-being—is keeping you in place, then, as I said earlier, you may be in for some hard times ahead. Worse yet, a small minority of faculty members feels that they have earned their position and that it is theirs to keep as long as they wish. If you feel this way, I can tell you that most of your colleagues will not agree with your sense of entitlement.

A sense of entitlement, stubbornness, and fear sometimes keeps us from making good decisions about when to retire. If you harbor these sorts of feelings, and especially if you act on them, you will stay in place at a cost: your reputation. It is a paradox that academics often squander their standing in their department, if not their field, by continuing to stay longer than they should because they do not know when and how to stop.

I have witnessed some ungraceful exits like Robert's and some even much worse. I have also seen that more than a few academics, reluctant to give up their position, come to regret holding on when they finally were forced to quit because they lacked the energy or health to go on. One of the foremost contributors in my area of research retained his position because he did not want to lose his office. He confessed to me a year after he finally stepped down at the age of eighty that if he had to do it over again, he would have left his position ten years earlier. His stubbornness and sense of not wanting to be pushed out led him to remain on the faculty even when he might have enjoyed his final decade of work more had he retired.

Knowing when to retire is one of the harder decisions that academics must make in the course of their careers. My advice and the approach that I adopted is to stop before your colleagues want you to retire, especially if you plan to continue working after you formally retire. There is a lot to be said for a graceful exit. In show business, the phrase for knowing when to get off the stage is "to leave them laughing." It is not a bad prescription for when to give up your own post.

PHASING OUT GRADUALLY

I don't want to claim that it is the Goldilocks solution to retirement, but many academics like to phase out gradually. I did this. When I turned sixty, I started to spend a semester away from the department each year. Not everyone can have the luxury of such a lengthy phase-out as I did. I had ample research funding that permitted me to teach half-time and write during the other half of the year; my university was flexible in permitting me to adopt this optimal schedule. Not all places would have found this arrangement acceptable, and not all departments would have been as generous as mine was. However, a growing number of colleges and universities are making it possible for tenured faculty to phase out gradually over a period of three to five years. I hope this practice continues, because it appears to work well according to most accounts. Of course, departments suffer to a certain extent if their senior faculty members are away as much as I was. I was acutely conscious of not doing my full share of department service and tried to do a bit more during the semesters when I was teaching. Still, I did not think that my colleagues were getting full value. That is why I retired at the relatively young age of sixty-eight in order to spend more time doing research and writing. I elected not to become emeritus because I did not want to send a signal to funders that I was no longer active and because I continue to supervise graduate students and postdocs.

Ironically, I discovered that I was immediately listed as an emeritus professor nonetheless. So much for my planning abilities!

Phasing out has a lot of advantages. First of all, you have some time to get used to the idea that you are not quite as indispensable as you might have believed. Life goes on when you are not around. One always hopes that colleagues will miss you when you are not there—but, as the old saying goes, graveyards are full of indispensable people. A gradual phase-out helps you get used to not making the day-to-day decisions that are the fabric of departmental life. It helps to see that others will make the decisions in your absence even if their calls are not always the same as yours might have been. In the preface, I introduced the concept of anticipatory socialization, the idea that it is often beneficial to practice roles before you actually assume them. Phasing out is a form of anticipatory socialization for the time when you fully retire.

BEYOND A POSITION

Not so long ago, I was giving a talk at a small faculty-student workshop that went on for several days. A colleague knew that I was writing a book on academic life and asked me to say a few words about it during one of the dinner sessions. In the course of doing so, I mentioned the topic of the final chapter of this book. After dinner, at the request of a prominent social scientist who had listened to my talk, I went for a walk to discuss questions he had about his endgame. The first question he asked happened to be the issue that had been very much on my mind several years earlier when I was thinking about retirement. "Will I find myself out in the cold if I give up my position?" It is a version of "Will you still need me, will you still feed me, when I am sixty-four?"

I told him what I had concluded before I took the plunge: "When you no longer have the professional props that we grow accustomed to in an academic position, it is very reassuring to discover that you still love what you do, you can keep on practicing your trade, and you can even still get invited to meetings like this one." I went on to tell him that "if, in fact, you stop being asked or stop wanting to do research and writing, then you know it is really time to stop." He understood immediately: ultimately academic life is about having a passion for ideas, doing research, and teaching others about the pursuit of knowledge.

Another of my close friends has written two important books since he retired that have given him immense satisfaction and a certain amount of recognition in areas of scholarly discourse that he had never dared to enter before he retired. He only dreamed about writing these books while he was still working because he lacked the time and, perhaps, the audacity to do so. He, too, felt liberated when he gave up his position.

Unlike some earlier phases of an academic career that are stressful and demanding, this period of post-retirement life can be highly pleasurable and rewarding. For the first time in your academic life, you are free to do pretty much what you want to do if you decide to keep on working and you can do it on your own schedule. As I said earlier, the trick is to peel off the parts of the job that you liked least and concentrate on the parts that you find most essential and satisfying. Perhaps for the first time in your life, you are able to spend your time exactly as you wish. Furthermore by lightening your load, you may find a surge of energy and a renewed sense of excitement. I know that I did.

Yes, there are some strings attached. If you continue to mentor students, then you cannot shirk writing letters of recommendations. If you promise to write a conference paper, you still face a deadline; and if you want to publish a paper, you still face critical reviews, revisions, and the boring tasks of reading and rereading your piece until it is as polished as you can make it. If you want to continue teaching, you must still prepare your classes and grade papers. But if this is what you most like doing more than anything else that you can think of, then you will probably not mind continuing to manage these arduous chores.

An anthropologist friend who retired some years ago was complaining to me that she never seemed to find time to finish the book that she had started many years before. It bothered her immensely because she continued to feel responsible for completing it. Feeling guilty, I told her, was not going to make her complete the volume. She had to want to do it, or otherwise it probably would never get done. I remember seeing a television interview with Arthur Schlesinger Jr., the great American historian, several years before he died. Then in his late eighties, he was discussing a new book that he had just written. The interviewer asked him if he was ever going finish the third book that he had planned to write on Franklin D. Roosevelt. Schlesinger smiled rather uncomfortably and replied, "I'm not sure that it will ever get done." I felt like shouting to the interviewer: "Give the poor man a break!"

The endgame of a scholarly life is, of course, finite and cannot go on indefinitely. There comes a time when you cannot climb the highest hills, so you settle for scaling those less steep or even staying on flat ground. The trick of managing life after a position, if your desire is to continue working, is to find satisfaction in what you are able to accomplish. The satisfaction of working is less motivated by the kind of drive and ambition that was required at earlier stages in your career, but by the sheer joy of learning, thinking, and, if it continues to suit you, writing or teaching. I can attest that it doesn't get any less fun. Governed as we often are by extrinsic rewards, academics can forget what got them into the business of academic life: a love of ideas, a sense of curiosity, and the challenge of discovery. When these activities are no longer gratifying, then and only then, you will know it is time to stop.

NOTES

PREFACE

1. U.S. Census Bureau, *2012 Statistical Abstract*, table 278, http://www.census .gov/compendia/statab/; National Center for Education Statistics (NCES), *Digest of Education Statistics* (2011), table 283 http://nces.ed.gov/programs/digest/d11/ tables/dt11_283.asp.

2. After many years of neglect, there is finally more attention devoted to the circumstances of those in the less desirable ranks of academia and more generally to the plight of adjunct faculty members who are often only weakly attached to the institutions for which they teach. See, for example, the advice column now in the *Chronicle of Higher Education* for adjuncts and many of the informative websites such as Joshua Boldt's *The Adjunct Project*: http://adjunctproject.com/.

3. *Inside Higher Education*, April 13, 2006.

4. Cathy Ann Trower, "Senior Faculty Satisfaction: Perceptions of Associate and Full Professors at Seven Public Research Universities." *TIAA-CREF Research Dialogue*, no. 101 (2011).; Paula Wasley, "Professors' Job Satisfaction Is Higher than Other Workers," *Chronicle of Higher Education*, November 16, 2007.

5. Pierre Bourdieu, "The Forms of Capital," in *Handbook of Theory and Research for the Sociology of Education*, ed. J. Richardson, 241–58 (New York: Greenwood Press, 1986).

6. I have benefited greatly from a long tradition of studies of academic life and higher education beginning with Thorstein Veblen, *The Higher Learning in America* (New York: Hill and Wang, 1918); Willard Waller, *The Sociology of Teaching* (New York: Wiley, 1932); Paul Félix Lazarsfeld and Wagner Thielens, *The Academic Mind: Social Scientists in Time of Crisis* (New York, Free Press, 1958); Theodore Caplow and Reece J. McGee, *The Academic Marketplace* (New York: Basic Books, 1958); David Mechanic, *Students Under Stress: A Study in the Social Psychology of Adaptation* (New York: Free Press of Glencoe, 1962); Burton R. Clark, *The Academic Life: Small World, Different Worlds* (Princeton, NJ: Princeton University Press, 1987); Diana Crane, *Invisible Colleges: Diffusion of Knowledge in Scientific*

Communities (Chicago: University of Chicago Press, 1988), to mention but a few of the classic studies of academia.

CHAPTER ONE

1. Keep in mind that these figures refer to applications and not individuals, so that any individual applying to several schools has a much better chance of acceptance in one or another program.

2. There is a well-accepted classification of universities carried out by the Council of Graduate Schools based on the intensity of research grants and scholarship. It has a fourfold ranking depending on the intensity of graduate research training: at the top are the most research-intensive universities (Tier 1), less research-intensive universities (Tier 2); other universities that grant doctoral degrees (Tier 3); colleges and universities without doctoral programs (Tier 4). This classification is sometimes used as a measure of quality or ranking, but it is not a perfect indicator of the quality of the institution or its resources. See Jeffrey R. Allum, Nathan E. Bell, and Robert S. Sowell, *Graduate Enrollment and Degrees: 2001 to 2011* (Washington, DC: Council of Graduate Schools, 2012); available at http://www.uccs.edu/Documents/ir/external%20reports/Graduate_Enrollment_and_Degrees_Report_2011_final.pdf.

3. Susan Aud et al., *The Condition of Education 2011* (NCES 2011–033), table 42–1, U.S. Department of Education, National Center for Education Statistics (Washington, DC: U.S. Government Printing Office, 2011); available at http://nces.ed.gov/pubs2011/2011033.pdf. A slightly different figure of 64,000 is cited by Allum, Bell, and Sowell, *Graduate Enrollment and Degrees: 2001 to 2011*.

4. National Science Foundation, Division of Science Resources Statistics, *Doctorate Recipients from U.S. Universities: 2011*, December 2012, NSF 13–301, Figure 1A The NSF survey uses a different methodology from the Council of Graduate Schools, which may account for the fact that it reports fewer doctorates awarded. According to their survey, about 50,000 degrees were conferred in 2011, a figure lower by 20 percent than is reported by the Council of Graduate Schools. See National Science Foundation, Division of Science Resources Statistics, *Doctorate Recipients from U.S. Universities: 2011*, See also Ronald G. Ehrenberg, Harriet Zuckerman, Jeffrey A. Groen, and Sharon Brucker, "How to Help Graduate Students Reach Their Destination," *Chronicle of Higher Education*, October 12, 2009.

5. National Science Foundation, Division of Science Resources Statistics, *Doctorate Recipients from U.S. Universities: 2009*, tables 28 and 33.

6. Tom W. Smith, "Job Satisfaction in the United States," NORC/University of Chicago, 2007. See also http://www.myplan.com/careers/top-ten/highest-job-satisfaction.php.

7. Piper Fogg, "A New Standard for Measuring Doctoral Programs," *Chronicle of Higher Education*, January 12, 2007. It is useful to consult the website http://sites .nationalacademies.org/PGA/Resdoc/

8. Nathan Kuncel, Sarah A. Hezlett, and Deniz S. Ones, "A Comprehensive Meta-Analysis of the Predictive Validity of the Graduate Record Examinations: Implications for Graduate Student Selection and Performance," *Psychological Bulletin* 127 (2011): 162–81.

9. National Science Foundation, Division of Science Resources Statistics, *Doctorate Recipients from U.S. Universities, 2011*.

10. Council of Graduate Schools (CGS), *Data Sources: Time-to-Degree for Doctorate Recipients* (Washington, DC: Council of Graduate Schools, 2010); reprinted from the March 2010 issue of the CGS *Communicator*, http://www.cgsnet.org/ck finder/userfiles/files/DataSources_2010_03.pdf.

11. David D. Perlmutter, "Your First Real Taste of Academic Culture," *Chronicle of Higher Education*, July 14, 2008.

12. James Lang, "Facing the Truth," *Chronicle of Higher Education*, May 12, 2008.

13. Sarah K. Goan and Alisa F. Cunningham, *Degree Completions in Areas of National Need 1996–97 and 2001–02* (NCES 2006–154), U.S. Department of Education (Washington, DC: National Center for Educational Statistics, 2006).

14. A good resource for the issues that arise in graduate school is the Pew Trusts Survey: Chris M. Golde and Timothy M. Dore, *At Cross Purposes: What the Experiences of Today's Doctoral Students Reveal about Doctoral Education* (Philadelphia: Pew Charitable Trusts, 2001); available at http://www.phd-survey.org/ report%20final.pdf.

15. Howard Becker, *Tricks of the Trade: How to Think about Your Research While You're Doing It* (Chicago: University of Chicago Press, 1998). Also see Pilar Mendoza, "Academic Capitalism and Doctoral Socialization: A Case Study," *Journal of Higher Education* 78, no. 1 (2007): 71–96.

16. See "What Makes Grad Students Graduate," *Inside Education*, December 6, 2005; and also "Why Grad Students Succeed or Fail," *Inside Education*, February 16, 2006.

17. David Mechanic, *Students under Stress: A Study in the Social Psychology of Adaptation* (Madison: University of Wisconsin Press, 1978).

18. Alfred Stanton and Morris Schwartz, *Mental Hospital* (New York: Basic Books, 2000).

19. Patricia Cohen, "In Economics Departments, a Growing Will to Debate Fundamental Assumptions," *New York Times*, July 11, 2007.

20. Scott Jaschik, "Finishing the Ph.D.," *Inside Higher Ed*, April 17, 2006; available at http://www.insidehighered.com/news/2006/04/17/yale.

21. Council of Graduate Schools, *Ph.D. Completion Project* (Washington, DC: Council of Graduate Schools, 2010); available at http://www.phdcompletion.org.

22. In the NSF report *Doctorate Recipients from U.S. Universities, 2011* that ex-

amined doctoral completions in 2011, the median length was eight years for scientists and engineers, nine years for social scientists, and about ten years for those in the humanities. In the field of education, the median length for completion of a PhD was twelve years.

CHAPTER TWO

1. "The Disposable Academic," *Economist*, December 16, 2010.

2. See Anthony T. Grafton and Jim Grossman, "A Very Modest Proposal for Graduate Programs in History," *Perspectives on History*, October 2011; available at http://www.historians.org/perspectives/issues/2011/1110/1110pre1.cfm.

3. Jean Waltman, Inger Bergom, Carol Hollenshead, Jeanne Miller, and Louise August, "Factors Contributing to Job Satisfaction and Dissatisfaction among Non-Tenure-Track Faculty," *Journal of Higher Education* 83, no. 3 (May/June 2012). See also Robin Wilson "Many Full-Time Instructors Prefer Working Off the Tenure Track," *Chronicle of Higher Education*, May 10, 2010; "A Portrait of Part-Time Faculty Members," *Coalition on the Academic Work Force*, June 2012; and Mary Ann Mason, Marc Goulden, and Karie Frasch, "Why Graduate Students Reject the Fast Track," *Academe*, January–February 2009; available at http://www.aaup.org/aaup/pubsres/academe/2009/jf/feat/maso.htm.

4. Kai Bird and Martin J. Sherman, *American Prometheus* (New York: Knopf, 2005).

5. See Alexandra M. Lord, "The Sweet Spot of a Nonacademic Job Search," *Chronicle of Higher Education*, January 2. 2012.

6. Christine Kelly, "Preparing for the Non-Academic Interview," *Inside Higher Ed*, May 29, 2009.

7. Alexandra Lord, "Every Ph.D. Needs a Plan B," *Chronicle of Higher Education*, March 16, 2009.

8. See *American Academic: The State of the Higher Education Workforce 1997–2007* (Washington, DC: American Federation of Teachers, 2009); available at http://www.aft.org/pdfs/highered/aa_highedworkforce0209.pdf. For a longer view of trends in faculty growth, see also *Trends in Faculty Status, 1975–2007* ; available at http://www.aaup2.org/research/TrendsinFacultyStatus2007.pdf.

9. Michael Stratford, "A Simple Spreadsheet Strikes a Nerve among Adjuncts," *Chronicle of Higher Education*, February 19, 2012.

10. Rob Jenkins, "The Community College Job Search," *Chronicle of Higher Education*, September 8, 2011.

11. Robin Matross Helms, *The New Challenges, New Priorities: The Experience of Generation X Faculty: A Study for the Collaborative on Academic Careers in Higher Education* (Cambridge, MA: COACHE at the Harvard University Graduate School of Education, 2010); available at http://isites.harvard.edu/fs/docs/icb.topic1023643.files/COACHE_GenX-NewChallengesNewPriorities_2010.pdf.

12. While there is no definitive study on the rate of publications, a number of studies indicate that a majority of PhDs do not publish at all. See, for example, Leo Mallette, "Publishing Rates of Graduated Education Ph.D. and Ed.D. Students," *Research in Higher Education* 2 (2009): 35–50; and Ellen Cohn, David Farrington, and Jon Sorensen, "Journal Publications of Ph.D. Graduates from American Criminology and Criminal Justice Programs: 1988–1997," *Journal of Criminal Justice Education* 11, no. 1 (2000): 35–49.

13. "Fifth Annual Survey: Great Colleges to Work For," *Chronicle of Higher Education*, August 5, 2012.

14. "Faculty and Staff Views," *Chronicle of Higher Education: Almanac of Higher Education 2009–2010* (2009), 27.

15. See Jerry A. Jacobs and Sarah E. Winslow, "The Academic Life Course, Time Pressures and Gender Inequality," *Community, Work and Family* 7, no. 2 (2004): 143–61; and "Stress and the Female Faculty Member," *Inside Higher Ed*, August 23, 2005.

16. Committee on Gender Differences in the Careers of Science, Engineering, and Mathematics Faculty, Committee on Women in Science, Engineering, and Medicine, Committee on National Statistics; National Research Council, *Gender Differences at Critical Transitions in the Careers of Science, Engineering, and Mathematics Faculty* (Washington, DC: National Academies Press, 2010).

17. See Gabriela Montell, "The (Sorry) State of Parental Leave in Academe," *Chronicle of Higher Education*, April, 22, 2010.

18. David Perlmutter, "When and How to Use the Other 'F' Word," *Chronicle of Higher Education*, March 18, 2010.

19. Beginning in the 1980s, commuter marriages became a topic of intense study by sociologists of the family. See Naomi Gerstel and Harriet Gross, *Commuter Marriage: A Study of Work and Family*,(New York: Guilford, 1984); Elaine A. Anderson and James W. Spruill, "The Dual-Career Commuter Family: A Lifestyle on the Move," *Marriage and Family Review* 19 (1993): 131–47; and Karla A. Bergen, Erika L. Kirby, and M. Chad McBride, "How Do You Get Two Houses Cleaned?" *Journal of Family Communication* 7 (2007): 291–311. A growing number of studies show the problems and adaptations of women and men in stable unions who live apart. This has also become a topic of much discussion in studies of academics. See, for example, Karen Miller-Loessi and Deborah Henderson, "Changes in American Society: The Context for Academic Couples," in *Academic Couples: Problems and Promises*, ed. Marianne A. Ferber and Jane W. Loeb (Chicago: University of Illinois Press, 1997), 25–43.

20. A thoughtful piece on academic marriages recently appeared: Elizabeth Simmons, "Dual-Career Academics: The Right Start, " *Inside Higher Education*, July 27, 2012.

21. "Full-Time Non-Tenure-Track Faculty," *Update* 2, no. 5 (September 1996); available at http://www.nea.org/assets/docs/HE/v2no5.pdf. See also James Soto and James Valadez, "Exploring the Satisfaction of Part-Time College Faculty in the United States," *Review of Higher Education* 26, no. 1 (2002): 41–56.

22. National Science Foundation, Division of Science Resources Statistics, *Doctorate Recipients from U.S. Universities: 2011*, National Science Foundation, December 2012, NSF 13–301.

23. Ibid., table 5C.

24. Kelly H. Kang, "NSF-NIH Survey of Graduate Students and Postdoctorates in Science and Engineering" (Arlington, VA: National Science Foundation and National Center for Science and Engineering Statistics, 2011); available at http://www.nsf.gov/statistics/srvygradpostdoc/.

25. See Phillip Sullivan, "Turning Down a Job You've Already Accepted," *Chronicle of Higher Education*, March 7, 2012.

CHAPTER THREE

1. James M. Lang, "Fare Thee Well, Year from Hell (Until Next Time)," *Chronicle of Higher Education*, May 6, 2010; available at http://chronicle.com/article/Fare-Thee-Well-Year-From-Hell/65354/.

2. Scott Jaschik, "Confidence Gap for New Profs," *Inside Higher Ed*, July 11, 2008.

3. John Lemuel, "The Welcome Mat," *Chronicle of Higher Education*, September 3, 2008.

4. Perceptions of preparation are reported in a study by the TIAA-CREF institution. Only about a third of faculty reported that they were "very effectively" prepared for teaching and research after graduate school, with men being more likely to report effective preparation than women. See "Confidence Gap for New Profs," *Inside Higher Ed*, July 11, 2008. See also Andrew Kemp, Samara Madrid, and Joseph Flynn, "Reflections on the First Year," *Chronicle of Higher Education*, July 17, 2008. A good source of young faculty members' attitudes about their jobs is the COACHE Survey conducted by the Harvard School of Education. See, for example, COACHE, *The Experience of Tenure-Track Faculty at Research Universities* (Cambridge, MA: Harvard University School of Education, 2010); available at http://deptchair.rice.edu/uploadedFiles/CAMP/Non-Rice_Resources/COACHE%20Assistant%20Prof%20Study.pdf.

5. Melissa Nicolas, "Lessons of an Academic Vagabond," *Inside Higher Ed*, January 20, 2010; available at http://www.insidehighered.com/advice/2010/01/20/nicolas.

6. The best and most recent survey on faculty satisfaction with job conditions and the tenure process was conducted by the Harvard Graduate School of Education's Collaborative on Academic Careers in Higher Education (COACHE). See the COACHE report on faculty views of the tenure process: *The Experience of Tenure-Track Faculty at Research Universities*. There are a number of high-quality representative sample surveys of academics conducted for various purposes and with different sponsors. The National Center on Educational Statistics has done

periodic surveys of professors in institutions of higher education. For an excellent account of faculty attitudes about their jobs based on the most comprehensive survey of faculty conducted by National Center on Educational Statistics in 2004. They report on a number of aspects of faculty life including departmental culture, work practices, and job attitudes. Emily Forrest Cataldi, Ellen M. Bradburn, and Mansour Fahimi, *2004 National Study of Postsecondary Faculty (NSOPF:04): Background Characteristics, Work Activities, and Compensation of Instructional Faculty and Staff: Fall 2003* (NCES 2006–176), U.S. Department of Education (Washington, DC: National Center for Education Statistics, 2005); available at http://nces.ed.gov/pubs2006/2006176.pdf. For earlier reports on the 1994 survey, there are two very good reports on views of faculty by Jack H. Schuster and Martin J. Finkelstein, *The American Faculty* (Baltimore: Johns Hopkins University Press, 2006); and Robert Seal Finkelstein and Jack H. Schuster, *The New Academic Generation* Baltimore: Johns Hopkins University Press, 1998).

7. See the COACHE study on *The Experience of Tenure-Track Faculty at Research Universities*, table 2.1.

8. There are some exceptions: see, for example, Michael J. Dooris and Marianne Guidos, "Tenure Achievement Rates at Research Universities," paper presented at the Annual Forum of the Association for Institutional Research (Chicago, May 2006); and *Gender Differences at Critical Transitions in the Careers of Science, Engineering, and Mathematics Faculty* (Washington, DC: National Academies Press, 2010).

9. Bill Reader, "Tenure Battle-Scarred," *Chronicle of Higher Education*, May 15, 2011.

10. National Science Foundation, Division of Science Resources Statistics, *Gender Differences in the Careers of Academic Scientists and Engineers: A Literature Review*, NSF 03–322, Project Officer, Alan I. Rapoport (Arlington, VA, 2003).

11. Robin Wilson, "Just Half of Professors Earn Tenure in 7 Years, Penn State Study Finds," *Chronicle of Higher Education*, July 21, 2006.

CHAPTER FOUR

1. These guesstimates are based on extrapolating from data reported in Jacobs and Winslow, who do not distinguish between faculty on and off the tenure track. Jerry A. Jacobs and Sarah E. Winslow, "The Academic Life Course, Time Pressures and Gender Inequality," *Community, Work and Family 7*, no. 2 (2004): 143–61. I also use information on the age at receipt of doctorate reported in Emily Forrest Cataldi, Ellen M. Bradburn, and Mansour Fahimi, *2004 National Study of Postsecondary Faculty (NSOPF:04) Report on Faculty and Instructional Staff: Fall 2003* (NCES 2006–176), U.S. Department of Education (Washington, DC: National Center for Education Statistics, 2005); available at http://nces.ed.gov/pubs2006/2006176.pdf.

2. Patricia Cohen, *In Our Prime: The Invention of Middle Age* (New York: Scribner, 2012).

3. Steve Jones, "It Is Tough All Over," *Chronicle of Higher Education*, May 6, 2008.

4. Kathryn D. Blanchard, "I've Got Tenure: How Depressing," *Chronicle of Higher Education*, January 31, 2012.

5. The demand for increased service may be one of the reasons why associate professors report somewhat lower levels of job satisfaction than either junior faculty or full professors. See, for example, Jeffrey Selingo, "A Midlife Crisis Hits College Campuses" *Chronicle of Higher Education*, July 18, 2008. The satisfaction level is relative because 86 percent of those in their late forties were satisfied with their jobs.

6. Scott Jaschik, "Disparate Burden," *Inside Higher Ed*, March 21, 2005; Modern Language Association, "Standing Still: The Associate Professor Survey," April 27, 2009; available at http://www.mla.org/pdf/cswp_final042909.pdf.

7. Audrey Williams June, "Not Moving on Up: Why Women Get Stuck at Associate Professor," *Chronicle of Higher Education*, April 27, 2009. See also COACHE, *The Experience of Tenure-Track Faculty Job Satisfaction Survey* (Cambridge, MA: Harvard University School of Education, 2010); available at http://deptchair.rice.edu/uploadedFiles/CAMP/Non-Rice_Resources/COACHE%20Assistant%20Prof%20Study.pdf.

8. According to the COACHE survey of faculty, there are relatively high levels of satisfaction with collaboration with faculty and satisfaction with department as a place to work. COACHE, *The Experience of Tenure-Track Faculty Job Satisfaction Survey*.

9. Annette Lareau, "The Gift of Obscurity: Advice for Emerging PhDs," *Footnotes* 25 (May/June 1997): 5.

10. James Soto Antony and James R. Valadez, "Exploring the Satisfaction of Part-Time College Faculty in the United States," *Review of Higher Education* 26, no. 1 (2002): 41–56.

11. For a balanced and useful report on the status of adjuncts, see *American Academic* 2 (March 2010).

12. Erik Erikson, *Childhood and Society* (New York: Norton, 1950).

13. Karen McElrath, "Gender, Career Disruption, and Academic Rewards," *Journal of Higher Education* 63, no. 3 (1992): 269–81. An analysis of faculty turnover using data from AAUP suggests that about one in ten faculty change positions or leave an institution for retirement each year: Ronald Ehrenberg, Hirschel Kasper, and Damiel Rees, "Faculty Turnover at American Colleges and Universities: Analyses of AAUP Data," *Economics of Education Review* 10, no. 2 (1991): 99–110.

14. COACHE, *The Experience of Tenure-Track Faculty Job Satisfaction Survey*.

15. Most studies of faculty satisfaction reveal remarkably little difference in the level of job contentment by type of institution or even whether faculty are full-time or part-time. See ibid. The most discontented academics are those who lack a

stable position and must piece together a livelihood by teaching across institutions as part-time adjuncts without the benefits of a full-time job.

CHAPTER FIVE

1. Daniel P. Kinney and Sharon P. Smith, "Age and Teaching Performance," *Journal of Higher Education* 63, no. 3 (1992): 282–302; Sharon G. Levin and Paula E. Stephan, "Research Productivity over the Life Cycle: Evidence for Academic Scientists," *American Economic Review* 81, no. 1 (1991): 114–32.

2. Many of the best surveys on faculty satisfaction show remarkably small differences by the level of research programs or the ranking of institutions. See, for example, the findings of COACHE that indicate that faculty satisfaction varies little by the Carnegie classification of research intensity. COACHE, *The Experience of Tenure-Track Faculty at Research Universities* (Cambridge, MA: Harvard University School of Education, 2010); available at http://deptchair.rice.edu/uploadedFiles/CAMP/Non-Rice_Resources/COACHE%20Assistant%20Prof%20Study.pdf. Cathy Ann Trower and Jared L. Bleak, *The Study of New Scholars: Tenure-Track Faculty Job Satisfaction Survey* (Cambridge, MA: Harvard Graduate School of Education, 2004); available at http://isites.harvard.edu/fs/docs/icb.topic1023643.files/SNS_report_insttype.pdf. Linda DeAngelo et al., *The American College Teacher: National Norms for the 2007–2008 HERI Faculty Survey* (Los Angeles: Higher Education Research Institute, UCLA, , 2009), table 6, p. 17; available at http://heri.ucla.edu/PDFs/pubs/briefs/brief-pr030508-08faculty.pdf.

3. Erik Erikson, *Childhood and Society* (New York: Norton, 1950).

4. For some useful information and accounts, see Julie Miller Vick and Jennifer S. Furlong, "Deciding When to Leave," *Chronicle of Higher Education*, April 14, 2011; Lorraine T. Dorfman et al., "Reactions of Professors to Retirement: A Comparison of Retired Faculty from Three Types of Institutions." *Research in Higher Education* 20, no. 1 (1984): 89–102; Thomas H. Benton, "14 Things to Do Before You Retire," *Chronicle of Higher Education*, November 6, 2006.

5. Valerie Martin Conley, "Retirement and Benefits: Expectations and Realities," in *The NEA 2007 Almanac of Higher Education* (Washington, DC: National Education Association, 2007); available at http://www.nea.org/home/32835.htm.

6. Audrey Williams June, "Professors Find Buyouts Are Not All about Money," *Chronicle of Higher Education*, May 30, 2010.

7. Sierra Millman, "Universities Take Varying Approaches to Retiring Faculty Members Study Finds," *Chronicle of Higher Education*, March 13, 2007.

8. Orley Ashenfelter and David Card, "Did the Elimination of Mandatory Retirement Affect Faculty Retirement?" *American Economic Review* 92, no. 4 (2002): 957–80.

INDEX

academic alternatives. *See* non-academic careers

academic career choice: availability of academic jobs, 39; desire to teach as a factor, 39–40; making the decision, 43; non-academic careers vs. (*see* non-academic careers); postdoc fellowships (*see* postdoctoral fellowships); reasons not to pursue, 41–43; reentering academic world after a non-academic job, 43–44; search for an academic position (*see* job search for an academic position); work-life balance and (*see* work-life balance)

academic meetings and conferences, 98–99, 138–40

academic midlife: average age at receipt of tenure, 113, 179n1; balancing academic and other work, 122–24; being realistic about your workload, 118–19; challenges of, 146–47, 180n14; characteristic dilemmas of, 114; conference attendance, 138–40; departmental and university service requirement, 120–22, 180n5; enjoying some ease due to experience, 119–20; managing multiple professional activities, 124–27; motivations for changing positions, 142–44; promotion to full professor, 140–42; range of reactions to the post-tenure experience, 115–17; reviewing papers and proposals, 137–38; suggestions for managing a move, 144–46; teaching and relations with students, 127–30; teaching at the graduate level, 130–36; typical academic mobility, 143, 180n12; writing recommendations, 136–37

application process for graduate school: decline in self-funding, 12; departments' tendency to accept applicants they know will come, 12; GRE scores, 10; number of schools to apply to, 13; personal statement, 11; recommendations, 11; undergraduate grades, 10–11; variations in the admissions process, 11–12

assistant professorship: circulating your work, 92–94; colleague relationships, 79–81, 178–79n6; conference and meetings attendance, 98–99; departmental and university service requirement, 81–84; department culture and, 76–79; etiquette for drawing from the work of others, 85; expanding your professional network, 96–98; perception of preparation for the job, 74–75, 178n4; reappointment and the road to tenure, 100–103; research and writing habit development, 89–94; skills to acquire for, 75; teaching load, handling, 84–89; tenure process (*see* tenure track); where to publish, 94–95; writing grant proposals, 96

Becker, Howard, 166

career of a graduate student: cumulative nature of, 31; decision to settle with a master's degree, 27; dissertation topic selection, 30–31; pre-doctoral examinations preparation, 28–29; process of specialization, 29–30; study groups and, 29

Collaborative on Academic Careers in Higher Education (COACHE), 178n6, 180n8

commuter unions, 54, 177n19

conference attendance, 98–99, 138–40

Council of Graduate Schools, 1

culture in academics: considerations for selecting a school, 15–16, 23–25; differences in perceptions of, 78; divide between academic and non-academic jobs, 44, 46; features that tend to be unique, 77; getting to know it by living it, 76, 78–79; teaching and relations with

to your future, 51–52; non-tenure-track positions, 46–47; number of unpublished PhDs, 50, 177n12; professional abuse of itinerant PhDs, 51; reasons not to pursue an academic career, 41–43; reasons to choose a lower-ranked institution, 48–49; reentering academic world after a non-academic job, 43–44; scope of fields available, 40–41, 45–46; work-life balance considerations, 49–50

online courses, 48
online journals, 94–95
Oppenheimer, Robert J., 43

personal readiness for graduate school: ability to manage stress and, 6–7; being honest about your level of passion, 6; being honest about your soft skills, 4–7
personal statement, 11
physical and biological sciences: collaboration with faculty and peers, 15, 24, 132; completion rates for dissertations, 32; disciplinary ideology considerations, 25–26; dissertation topic selection, 30; job availability, 39, 56; length of time required to obtain a doctorate, 3; non-academic careers, 45; postdoctoral fellowships, 58; promotion to full professor, 140–41; publishing record and, 107; social nature of ideas in the field, 131; time to finish a degree, 175–76n22
Population Association of America, 114, 158
postdoctoral fellowships: giving indications of scholarly promise, 60; matriculation to by field, 58; opportunities for work, 58–59; planning your agenda during, 59–60; value of collaboration, 60–61; what to look for in a program, 59; what you can expect to accomplish, 60
pre-doctoral examinations preparation, 28–29
professional network: attending academic meetings and conferences, 98–99, 138–40; collaborations and coauthorship situations, 131–36; colleague relationships, 79–81, 178–79n6; expanding as an assistant professor, 96–98
publishing record: impact on a job search, 56–58; where to publish as an assistant professor, 94–95

recommendations: for graduate applications, 11; writing for students, 136–37
research and writing habit development: developing a pipeline of production, 93–94;

helpfulness of routines, 90–91; saving editing for last, 91–92; tenure-track requirements, 90; time management and, 89–90
retirement. *See* senior academics
Riley, Matilda, 166

scholarly identity, 29–30
school selection: culture of the department and, 15–16, 23–25; financial support offered, 16–18; ranking of programs, 2, 8–9, 174n2; record of placement of graduates, 14; time to finish a degree as a consideration, 13–14
senior academics: decision to not retire, 165–68; decision to phase out gradually, 168–69; decision to retire completely, 162–65; drawbacks of retirement, 163; factors affecting the retirement decision, 158; generativity and, 157–59; how to know when it is time to stop, 166–67; lack of literature on the retirement process, 157; loving what you do and, 169–71; range of feelings about retirement, 161–62; seniority and its meanings, 149–50; status of older academics, 150–51; Supreme Court decision on retirement age, 164; taking on new challenges and, 155–56, 181n2; work life of a senior academic, 152–54
social sciences: collaboration with faculty and peers, 15, 24, 132–33; completion rates for dissertations, 32; disciplinary ideology considerations, 25–26; dissertation topic selection, 30; job availability, 39, 56; length of time required to obtain a doctorate, 3; non-academic careers, 45; postdoctoral fellowships, 58; promotion to full professor, 140–41; publishing record and, 107; social nature of ideas in the field, 131; time to finish a degree, 175–76n22
soft skills needed for graduate school, 4–7
students. *See* teaching and relations with students; teaching at the graduate level
Supreme Court, US, 164

TAs (teaching assistants), 17
teaching: gaining confidence in, 86–87; managing dissertation oversight commitments, 88–89; managing interactions with students, 87–88; tips for managing, 85–86; typical loads, 84–85
teaching and relations with students: adjunct faculties' role in teaching, 129–30; culture of the department and, 127–28; teaching undergraduates, 128–29
teaching assistants (TAs), 17

teaching at the graduate level: collaboration and coauthorships with students, 130–31, 134–35; range of preferences regarding desired interactions, 130; tricks to handling a large load of students, 131

tenure track: average age at receipt of tenure, 113, 179n1; considerations when tenure is denied, 111–12; the department review, 108–9; evaluating your reviews, 101; job change considerations, 101–3; non-tenure-track positions appeal, 46–47; period after achieving (*see* senior academics); period before achieving (*see* assistant professorship); petitions for review of the decision, 110; proportion of academic positions on a tenure track, 104; range of reactions to the post-tenure experience, 115–17; rate of success, 110; reasons not to pursue, 42–43; research and writing habit development, 90; role of departmental politics, 108; the second review, 109; start of the process of evaluation, 104–5; steps in the review process, 105–7; stressfulness of, 103; the third review, 109–10; typical timeline, 100; understanding how you are meeting expectations, 100–101

terms of employment negotiation, 69–71

TIAA-CREF, 178n4

time management: developing a decision matrix, 126–27; in graduate school, 22–23; potential for overcommitment, 124–25; research and writing habit development, 89–90; suggestions for budgeting your time, 125–26; tips for your dissertation writing schedule, 34–35

women: applications to graduate school, 1; considerations on when to start a family, 52–53, 54–55; protecting against offensive behavior, 80; tendency to accept too many requests for service, 121–22

work-life balance: considerations for commuter unions, 54, 177n19; considerations for selecting a career, 49–50; considerations for single parents, 53–54; considerations for women, 52–53, 54–55; generally good and bad times to start a family, 52; during postdoctoral period, 54; time management (*see* time management)